D1738163

Movement

and

Modernism

Movement
and
Modernism

Yeats,
Eliot,
Lawrence,
Williams,
and Early
Twentieth-
Century
Dance

Terri A. Mester

The University
of Arkansas Press
Fayetteville 1997

01 00 99 98 97   5 4 3 2 1

Designed by Liz Lester

☻ The paper used in this publication meets the minimum requirements of the American National Standard for Permanence of Paper for Printed Library Materials Z39.48-1984.

Library of Congress Cataloguing-in-Publication Data

Mester, Terri A.
  Movement and modernism : Yeats, Eliot, Lawrence, Williams, and early twentieth-century dance / Terri A. Mester.
    p.   cm.
  Includes bibliographical references and index.
  ISBN 1-55728-455-5 (alk. paper)
  1. English literature—20th century—History and criticism. 2. Dance in literature. 3. Yeats, W. B. (William Butler), 1865–1939—Knowledge—Dance. 4. Eliot, T. S. (Thomas Stearns), 1888–1965—Knowledge—Dance. 5. Lawrence, D. H. (David Herbert), 1885–1930—Knowledge—Dance. 6. Williams, William Carlos, 1883–1963—Knowledge—Dance. 7. American poetry—20th century—History and criticism. 8. Modernism (Literature)—Great Britain. 9. Modernism (Literature)—United States. 10. Modern dance—History—20th century. 11. Dance—History—20th century. I. Title.
PR478.D35M47   1997
820.9'357—dc21

96-29802
CIP

Selections from "Nineteen Hundred and Nineteen" and "Among School Children" reprinted with the permission of Simon & Schuster from *The Poems of W. B. Yeats: A New Edition,* edited by Richard J. Finneran. Copyright © 1928 by Macmillan Publishing Company, renewed 1956 by Georgie Yeats.

Selections from "Byzantium" reprinted with the permission of Simon & Schuster from *The Poems of W. B. Yeats: A New Edition,* edited by Richard J. Finneran. Copyright © 1933 by Macmillan Publishing Company, renewed 1961 by Bertha Georgie Yeats.

Selections from *Four Quartets,* copyright © 1943 by T. S. Eliot and renewed 1971 by Esme Valerie Eliot, reprinted by permission of Harcourt Brace & Company.

Selections from "The Love Song of J. Alfred Prufrock," "The Waste Land," and "Cousin Nancy" in *Collected Poems 1909–1962* by T. S. Eliot, copyright © 1936 by Harcourt Brace & Company, copyright © 1963, 1964 by T. S. Eliot, reprinted by permission of the publisher.

Selections from William Carlos Williams's *Paterson,* copyright © 1946, 1948, 1958 by William Carlos Williams; *Collected Poems 1909–1939,* vol. 1, copyright © 1938 by New Directions Publishing Corporation; *Collected Poems 1939–1962,* vol. 2, copyright © 1944, 1948, 1962 by William Carlos Williams; and *Kora in Hell,* copyright © 1957 by William Carlos Williams, reprinted by permission of New Directions Publishing Corporation.

Selections from *The Cantos of Ezra Pound,* copyright © 1968 by Ezra Pound, reprinted by permission of New Directions Publishing Corporation.

In memory of my father, Lou J. Federman

Acknowledgments

This project was born the day I decided to try synthesizing two of my great passions in life: dance and literature. I would like to thank some of the professors in the English and dance departments at Case Western Reserve University who helped make this possible. First, Bill Marling, who in addition to his indefatigable efforts at editing this manuscript, instilled in me a deep appreciation for modernist poetry. Thanks also to Roger Salomon and P. K. Saha for their invaluable advice and criticism on the Yeats, Williams, and Lawrence chapters. I would also like to thank Kathy Karipides and Kelly Holt of the dance department at Case for allowing me to take their technique classes and for their warmhearted commitment to my undertaking. Thanks also to Dean Robert Holland at the University of Akron's Honors College and to my friend and mentor Lou Giannetti at CWRU for encouraging me to write.

I would also like to thank Monica Moseley and Charles Perrier of the Dance Collection at the New York Public Library for assisting me in the selection of photographs and my editor, Kevin Brock, at the University of Arkansas Press for being kind and personable throughout the publication process.

Most of all, I am indebted to my family—Tom, Jonathan, and Nick—for their infinite patience and support.

Contents

Illustrations

Abbreviations

Auto	Yeats, *Autobiographies*
CP	Yeats, *The Collected Poems of W. B. Yeats*
CP1	Williams, *The Collected Poems of William Carlos Williams.* Vol. 1: 1909–39
E & I	Yeats, *Essays and Introductions*
Imag	Williams, *Imaginations*
LCL	Lawrence, *Lady Chatterley's Lover*
Phx	Lawrence, *Phoenix: The Posthumous Papers of D. H. Lawrence*
Phx II	Lawrence, *Phoenix II: Uncollected, Unpublished, and Other Prose Works*
R	Lawrence, *The Rainbow*
SL	Williams, *The Selected Letters of William Carlos Williams*
SP	Eliot, *Selected Poems*

Introduction:
The Theoretical/
Historical Context

Literary historians have left us many studies that trace fertilization among the arts as they entered modernism. According to one, the interfusing "not only among the separate nations of Europe (and America) but also among the various arts of literature, music, painting, and sculpture, was on a scale as never before" (Bradbury and McFarlane 201). The influence of cinematic montage, for example, on Virginia Woolf, James Joyce, and William Faulkner has been analyzed, as has cubist and dadaist technique in Wallace Stevens and William Carlos Williams. But only a handful of critics have written at any length on the impact of dance on literary modernism, even though dance, too, met the new century with some profound innovations.[1] Ballet was revolutionized and a totally new genre—the modern dance—was invented.

No matter how many radical innovations the dance underwent, the notion that it could be part of the intellectual history of the period seemed an absurdity for some time. First, it was largely perceived as a marginal, frivolous "women's" art.[2] Second, dance's corporeality challenged the dominant ethical and religious ideology of Western society, which in many ways depended on repressions of the body. Some intellectuals, moreover, shunned dance because of its inherent ephemerality. Speaker "B" in T. S. Eliot's

"A Dialogue on Dramatic Poetry" expresses this idea when he simultaneously praises the ballet for concerning "itself with a permanent form" and discredits it for concerning "itself with the ephemeral in content" (*Selected Essays* 34). A poem, the theory seems to have been, could last forever, while the dance existed only at the vanishing point. Third, dance and literature were particularly uneasy bedfellows, for writers and dancers were said to possess antithetical sensibilities. Narratives of dancers' private lives have left us with the stereotypical narcissistic image of a female or homosexually-bound male thwarted intellectually at an early age by long years of grueling physical training in front of a mirror. On the other hand, what could practitioners of a *living* art that dispensed with words possibly have in common with the stereotypical poet, bent over an ink-stained table, burning midnight oil, and endlessly "stitching and unstitching" a line or two?

Yet if the new dance had no effect on modernism, as the dearth of critical commentary might seem to indicate, how does one account for the prevalence of dance imagery in the works of four key modernists: W. B. Yeats, T. S. Eliot, D. H. Lawrence, and William Carlos Williams? Based on a mix of mythical and actual sources, including the androgynous Hindu dancing god Shiva, the decadent Salomé, American dancers Loïe Fuller and Ruth St. Denis, and some significant lovers, Yeats's dancer is usually a female who appears in the great metaphysical poems of the 1920s as his supreme symbol for unity of being. Williams, on the other hand, frequently dramatizes himself as a lusty dancer in his poetry. Dancing, especially in *Paterson,* is Williams's foremost figure for the imagination. Early in his career, Eliot created the disturbing image of a saintly dancer mortifying his flesh in the desert to become a "dancer before God." Later, in *Four Quartets,* he disembodied the dance into a process of religious transcendence. In between, his lost souls plod rhythmically around in debased rituals, such as the "prickly pear" section of "The Hollow Men." Although the dance is absent from his poetry, Lawrence wrote a highly rhythmical prose that mimetically approximated it in language. The dance scenes in his major fiction consist either of women dancing alone as an expression of psychic imbalance or of men and women dancing harmoniously as an expression of "phallic consciousness." In either case, the dance enabled Lawrence to unearth the deeper, impersonal self buried beneath the "old stable *ego* of the character."

These four modernists saw in dance a mirror of their own preoccupations. They were either influenced by or shared the same artistic concerns as ballet dancer/choreographers Mikhail Fokine, Vaslav Nijinsky, and Léonide Massine and such precursors of modern dance as Ruth St. Denis, Isadora Duncan, and Loïe Fuller. Yeats, for example, drew his inspiration from the contemporary craze for Oriental dances, which included everything from St. Denis's mystical solos and Fokine's exotic ballets to the public's insatiable appetite for treacherous *femmes fatales*. Several of Eliot's poems allude to ballets that are indissolubly linked with Nijinsky, and in his critical writings he repeatedly singled out Massine for the latter's exemplary "moral training" and self-sacrifice to ballet's unified point of view and four-hundred-year-old tradition, in which the past existed simultaneously in the present. Williams, at the other extreme, found in Duncan's rebellion against a restrictive, European form an analogue for his desire to forge a new American poetry (Mariani 67). Lawrence never saw Duncan perform, but shared with the dancer an anatomical view of human psychology, which privileged the solar plexus as the primary center of "blood consciousness," or one's sympathetic awareness of the universe. And like Duncan, both Lawrence and Williams spent a lifetime rebelling against Puritan morality.

Through the influence of French symbolism and Italian futurism, these modernists became aware of connections between the dance's formal properties and their own art. As a preverbal activity, dance suggested several paradigms for verbal artists wishing to "make it new," including a "primitive" unity between dancer and dance through the dancer's "impersonality." All four writers studied nontheatrical, primordial dance rituals in an attempt to recover something they thought lost to the modern world.

Yeats, Eliot, Lawrence, and Williams were by no means the only modernists to be touched by the new dance. Americans Hart Crane, John Dos Passos, and E. E. Cummings were avid dance aficionados. Hart Crane paid homage to Isadora Duncan's steadfast adherence to artistic ideals in the "Quaker Hill" section of *The Bridge*. John Dos Passos wrote a brief biographical segment on her in his trilogy *USA*, in which the dancer personified Art in an era of big money and crass commercialism (Ludington 306). Commissioned by his friend, balletomane Lincoln Kirstein, E. E. Cummings wrote a ballet scenario based on *Uncle Tom's Cabin* for former Ballets Russes choreographer George Balanchine and his new American Ballet Company.

On the other side of the Atlantic members of the Bloomsbury circle frequently note in memoirs and diaries their attending performances to see Nijinsky and Karsavina, to hear the music of Stravinsky and Prokoviev, and later to see the sets and costumes of Picasso and Matisse. Leonard Woolf, for instance, perceived that dance was at the forefront of the "profound changes" taking place in London in 1911. In *Beginning Again,* he recalled his excitement after being away as a civil servant in Ceylon for seven years:

> Freud and Rutherford and Einstein were at work beginning to revolutionize our knowledge of our own minds and of the universe. . . . In literature one seemed to feel the ominous lull before the storm which was to produce in a few years *A La Recherche du Temps Perdu, Ulysses,* "Prufrock" and *The Waste Land, Jacob's Room* and *Mrs. Dalloway.* In painting we were in the middle of the profound revolution of Cezanne, Matisse and Picasso. . . . And to crown all, night after night we flocked to Covent Garden, entranced by a new art, a revelation to us benighted British, the Russian Ballet in the greatest days of Diaghilev and Nijinsky. (37)

Forty years later, E. M. Forster vividly recalled "Nijinsky's leap in *Le Spectre de la rose,* the first London performance of *Le Sacre du printemps* and the drop curtain of *Schéhérazade*" (4). Virginia Woolf, Lytton Strachey, and Rupert Brooke all caught ballet fever, and John Maynard Keynes married Lydia Lopokova, one of Ballets

Russes's prima ballerinas (Garafola 316–20). But satisfied with their intuitive understanding, these intellectuals refrained from analyzing how the new dance had touched their imaginations. Unwittingly, they contributed to subsequent impressions that the dance, in so far as it contributed to modernism, was a vanishing act.

The Background: Dramatizing Primitive Myth

In order to understand what "entranced" the Bloomsbury crowd and the four modernists who are the subjects of subsequent chapters, it is necessary to briefly note a few of the major happenings in dance in the early part of the century. One of the crossroads where the new dance and modernism met was in the portrayal of "primitive" myths, rituals, and archetypes—like the Racial Other and Eternal Feminine. Included in this category are Duncan's *Mother,* St. Denis's *Radha,* Mikhail Fokine's pseudo-Oriental ballets for the Ballets Russes like *Schéhérazade,* and later in the 1930s Martha Graham, Mary Wigman, and Doris Humphrey's archetypal dances like *Primitive Mysteries, Sacrifice,* and *With My Red Fire.* Nijinsky's *Le Sacre du printemps,* in its sacrifice of a Chosen Maiden and primeval evocation of prehistoric Russia, was unquestionably the most famous dance in this genre and became virtually synonymous with the idea of modernity. Who is not familiar with its legendary Paris premiere in 1913, which caused one of the greatest furors in French theatrical history? Fighting broke out and the music was all but drowned in the hubbub.

The original ballet, unfortunately, was a casualty of dance's "inherent ephemerality" and vanished after eight performances. Nijinsky's impersonal form and profound innovations in movement were lost to posterity when his erstwhile lover Diaghilev fired him from the Ballets Russes for marrying the Hungarian ballerina Romola de Pulska. When the company revived the ballet after World

"Adolescents" from Nijinsky's original version of *Le Sacre du printemps* (Paris, 1913). "Living beings cling to each other . . . lost among the horrible indifference of society." *Courtesy of the Dance Collection, New York Public Library for Performing Arts, Astor, Lenox, and Tilden Foundations.*

War I, Diaghilev replaced Nijinsky's modernist choreography with Massine's conventionally romantic movements. Since that time, over sixty different versions of the ballet have been performed, including Millicent Hodson's scholarly reconstruction of the original for the Joffrey Ballet in 1987. In light of the work's history, one can understand why a literary critic like Herbert Howarth would note the influence of Stravinsky's dissonant score on the "method" of that quintessentially modernist document *The Waste Land* and conspicuously ignore Nijinsky's name and contributions (234).

While it is true that Stravinsky's music was the most uncompromising of his compositions at the time, Nijinsky had the difficult task of decoding its rhythmic complexity. For help, Diaghilev turned to Emile Jaques-Dalcroze, a Swiss musician who, at his institute near Dresden, had devised a system called "eurythmics" based on exercises to reproduce increasingly complex patterns of rhythm or beats in the body.[3] Nijinsky transplanted whole segments of Dalcroze's exercises into *Le Sacre*. Reports indicate that the movement resembled the involuntary condition of trance: the dancers shook, trembled, shivered, and stamped convulsively. Lincoln Kirstein likened it to an "apocalyptic epilepsy hypnotizing a community of ecstatic spastics" (144). The French critic Jacques Rivière described the horror of the depersonalized mass depicted in the ballet.

> We find ourselves in the presence of man's movements at a time when he did not yet exist as an individual. Living beings still cling to each other; they exist in groups, in colonies, in shoals; they are lost among the horrible indifference of society. . . . Their faces are devoid of any individuality. At no time during the dance does the Chosen Maiden show the personal terror that ought to fill her soul. She carries out a rite; she is absorbed by a social function, and without any sign of comprehension or of interpretation, she moves as dictated by the desires and impulses of a being vaster than herself. (quoted, Kirstein 168)

Interestingly, *Le Sacre*'s graphic depiction of a ritualized female sacrifice had no precedent in either Slavic mythology or ballet tradition. Even in Frazer's descriptions of universal vegetation rites, the male gods (like Attis and Osiris) are always the ones slain and sacrificed. And while nineteenth-century romantic ballets like *Swan Lake* and *Giselle* conclude with a female sprite's death, she is a sacrifice to love rather than the prevailing social order, and her demise occurs quietly, decorously offstage.

Nijinsky's ballet, however, did set a precedent for modernist literary texts. Eliot's *Sweeney Agonistes* hints at dark, secret connections between sex and sacrifice, and Lawrence's "The Woman Who Rode Away" concludes with an eroticized scene of ritualized female sacrifice. More generally, *Le Sacre*'s dark vision of a primal past, like *The Waste Land,* was a figure for modern life, especially its barbarism and savagery. It anticipated the evils of war and a depersonalized society ruled by the machine and was a harbinger of the dark, Dionysian forces discerned under the veneer of Victorian civility, whether they were called the unconscious (Freud), the dark gods (Lawrence), or the Sidhe (Yeats).

The Lure of the Orient

The depiction of primitive myth was not the only common ground between literary modernism and dance. Many artists, disillusioned with their Christian humanist heritage, looked to the Orient for alternate spiritual values. Eliot's *The Waste Land* had its Oriental aspects, such as Buddha's "Fire Sermon" and the Sanskrit of the last section, just as Pound had his Cathay poems and the ideogram. Yeats's lifelong preoccupation with Eastern literature and philosophy resulted in his Noh plays, his translations of the *Upanishads,* and the speculations of *A Vision.* The cult of the East was no less popular as a cultural phenomena. The mania for Oriental things in the decorative arts, for example, contributed to the exotic, curvilinear lines of art nouveau. The Eastern trend, however, was most conspicuous in dance, where two of its innovators, Fokine and St. Denis, captured an Orient of the imagination, if not of reality.

Fokine's Eastern ballets—*Cléopâtre* (1909), the "Polovtsian Dances" from *Prince Igor* (1909), and *Le Dieu blue* (1912)—established the Ballets Russes in the public mind as the most exciting and important artistic enterprise in the first decades of the century.[4] If the styles of these ballets were not strictly Egyptian, Hindu, or Tartar, neither were they strictly classical (Jowitt 108). Influenced by Isadora Duncan's visit to St. Petersburg in 1905, Fokine reformed the classical tradition from within by choreographing more expressive and natural movement. A Fokine ballet, moreover, was a feast for the senses; the continual interlacing of wavelike movement with the decor, lighting, and costumes, according to one French critic, created "unknown relationships in the mind" (Priddin 106). *Schéhérazade* (1910), the premiere crowd pleaser in the company's first seasons, combined Leon Bakst's art nouveau sets, with their opulent, glittering, luxurious curves and bold color combinations, and the rich sonorities of Rimsky-Korsakov's nationalistic music, unheard in the West. What most thrilled audiences, however, was the notorious orgy scene, the impact of which Serge Grigoriev, Diaghilev's *regisseur,* attributed not to its voluptuous-

Nijinsky's Favorite Slave from the Ballets Russes production of Fokine's Oriental fantasy, *Schérérazade* (around 1910). *Courtesy of the Dance Collection, New York Public Library for Performing Arts, Astor, Lenox, and Tilden Foundations.*

ness, but rather to its variety of dances and its timing: the scene reached a great climax, came to a halt, and then unwound (Spencer 46). The ballet's lead dancer, Zobeïda, the sultan's wife, was a variation of the *femme fatale,* or predatory female, who fused the Eternal Feminine with the Racial Other and posed a real threat to Western, historically determined, patriarchal society.[5]

Not every depiction of the Orient in dance was meant to be erotic or sensational. Ruth St. Denis, a young American from New Jersey, evoked its mystical side in her unashamedly inauthentic renditions of various Eastern deities. With a hodge-podge background made up of bits of ballet, acrobatics, and François Delsarte's analysis of body gestures, St. Denis was largely a self-made dancer. She supported herself with acting parts when she could not find dancing engagements. While touring with the David Belasco Company's production of *Dubarry* in the early part of the century, St. Denis's "destiny as a dancer sprung alive" (as she later wrote in her autobiography). She and a friend were seated at a soda fountain in Buffalo when she suddenly glanced up and noticed an advertisement for Egyptian cigarettes. Riveted by an image of the Egyptian goddess Isis in the poster, St. Denis knew she would "become a rhythmic and impersonal instrument of spiritual revelation" (52). St. Denis, however, was always inclined toward the mystical and maintained a lifelong interest in Christian Science, American Transcendentalism, and Hindu philosophy.

Radha was the first dance to come out of her "conversion" and remained her signature piece. As *Radha,* the milkmaid and consort of the Hindu god Krishna, St. Denis—barefoot and resplendent in a scanty costume made of jewels—began by abandoning herself to the seductive "Dance of the Five Senses," which expressed the sensual joys of human existence. Then, overcome by the futility of the joys of the flesh, she ended the dance seated in the lotus position in chaste, trancelike contemplation. Whether or not audiences understood the religious connotations (that her earthly passion for Krishna symbolized a desire for union with the Absolute), they responded enthusiastically to St. Denis's beauty and the quality of her dancing, especially her undulating arms and intricate hand gestures. *Radha* was immediately successful in its first showing in New York in 1906 and led to further solo recitals in London, Paris, Vienna, and several cities in Germany. Other pseudo-Oriental dances quickly followed, like *Nautch, Cobra, Egypta,* and *Incense.*

Like the other two forerunners of modern dance, Fuller and Duncan, St. Denis became the darling of intellectuals. Yeats and Shaw helped sponsor her first London tour; the American architect Stanford White and Germans Count Harry Kessler and director Max Reinhardt became fervent admirers. The Austrian symbolist poet Hugo von Hofmannsthal became her close friend. The immediacy of her dancing inspired Hofmannsthal's essay "The Incomparable Dancer," published in 1906. He detected the

A mystical vision of the Orient in *Radha* (1906), Ruth St. Denis's signature piece. *Courtesy of the Dance Collection, New York Public Library for Performing Arts, Astor, Lenox, and Tilden Foundations.*

spirit of modernism in her art and felt her dances would have been impossible "in an age less sophisticated, less complex than ours." He described her choreography as "thoroughly strange."

> It is not seeking for meditation, for being bridged over. It will have nothing to do with cultivation; it will not illustrate, will not elucidate. It presents us with something totally strange, without pretending to be ethnographic or sensational. It is there simply for the sake of its beauty. (quoted, Shelton 69–70)

Hofmannsthal was supposed to collaborate with St. Denis and Max Reinhardt on a new poetic treatment of the biblical dancer Salomé along the lines of Oscar Wilde's scenario, but this never materialized (Jowitt 125). St. Denis had objected to Wilde's version because it relegated the dancing to a secondary role, and she typically put off creating her own version of the legendary dancer until 1933 (Shelton 76–77).

Among the group of exotic, treacherous females like Fokine's Zobeïda, Salomé reigned supreme. Dancers as diverse as Anna Pavlova, Maud Allan, and Mati Hari brought this archetypal *femme fatale* to life in vaudeville and on the legitimate stage during the years just before World War I, when the appetite for exotica peaked. Salomé would also be a definitive influence on the image of the dancer in Yeats, Eliot, and Lawrence.

The Revolt against Puritan Morality

As the dance grew into a serious, legitimate art form, from *Schéhérazade*'s orgy of sex and violence to *Radha*'s seductive spiritualism, it was communicating increasingly subversive messages about sexuality to a generation eager to free itself of Victorian stuffiness. Because the meanings of gestures were more ambiguous than the written word, choreographers as a rule enjoyed greater impunity from censorship than writers did. Nijinsky, for example, could suggest lesbianism and masturbation in *L'Après-midi d'un faune* (1912) and a *ménage à trois* in *Jeux* (1913),[6] while the censors not only suppressed but threatened to burn every existent copy of *The Rainbow* for Lawrence's portrayal of a nude pregnant woman dancing alone in her bedroom.

Isadora Duncan, who never shied away from dancing when pregnant, enjoyed taunting audiences with her freer, uninhibited movement, scanty costumes, and blatant sexuality. Her independence and freedom became a sort of symbolic reference. Even before the public saw her perform, they were aware of her well publicized, scandalous lifestyle, which included two children born out of wedlock, bouts of alcoholism, and a lengthy flirtation with Russian communism. In the early 1920s Duncan, with her hair dyed fiery red, shocked prim and proper Bostonians by dancing uncorseted and baring a breast at the climax in response to jeers from the audience. Just to provoke them further, she would lecture from the stage on

Isadora Duncan, typically
clad in bare feet and tunic.
*Courtesy of the Dance
Collection, New York Public
Library for Performing Arts,
Astor, Lenox, and Tilden
Foundations.*

the brave new world of Soviet Russia, often accompanied by her
belligerent, drunken husband (over twenty years her junior), the
poet Sergei Essenin. When Duncan repeated her Boston concert in
Cleveland in 1922, a young Hart Crane sat mesmerized in the audience. Later, he described the event as "a wave of life, a flaming gale
that passed over the heads of the nine thousand in attendance."
According to Crane, Duncan remained oblivious to the audience's
jeers and catcalls and told them afterwards to go home and read
Calamus, although the poet was doubtful that anyone in the audience had ever heard of Whitman (109).

Ironically, Duncan danced in bare feet and loose, free-
flowing tunics more for moral than aesthetic reasons. Her choice of
costume expressed her desire to liberate women from their psycho-
logically confining role in Victorian society. Her ideal was to see
women living their lives to the fullest, unhampered by restrictive

clothing and social conventions. Probably by no coincidence, the area the corset affected most, the solar plexus, became the focal point of Duncan's aesthetic and one of Lawrence's central tenets as well. In her autobiography, Duncan refers to this region as "the central spring of all movement, the crater of motor power, the unity from which all diversions of movement are born" (*My Life* 72). Lawrence called the solar plexus "the great sympathetic center" in which we feel our unity with the universe (*Fantasia* 36).

French Symbolism and the Internalization of Dance: Mallarmé's Nonwoman/Nondancing Ballerina

In addition to converging interests and aspirations, modernists also regarded some of the dance's formal properties as desirable models for a new poetry. They saw, for instance, in the dancer's endless struggle to achieve perfection of line, an analogue for their own emphasis on the hard, dry presentation of the poetic image. The French symbolist poet Stéphane Mallarmé was the first to isolate some of these correspondences in a few influential essays written on dance at the end of the nineteenth century, which were later paraphrased and expanded by his disciple Paul Valéry. Basically, Mallarmé noticed that the dancer epitomized the modern characteristic of "impersonality" in art and that her movements constituted an unwritten language in some ways superior to the written word. And because her female beauty was objectified into dazzling, evocative symbols, the dancer became the visual incarnation of Mallarmé's notion of the Ideal.

To fully understand Mallarmé's attraction to dance, however, it is first necessary to isolate a few characteristics of symbolism and its link to modernism. Mallarmé worshipped an ideal of gratuitous beauty that was mystical. His ideal, or *"Idée,"* was analogous to Platonic forms in that it could not be apprehended empirically through the senses. Instead of Plato's postulate of One

Supreme Being which transcended all forms, Mallarmé's ultimate reality was Absolute Beauty. In trying to attain his ideal, according to C. M. Bowra, he "convey[ed] a supernatural experience in the language of visible things and therefore every word is a symbol and is used not for its common purposes—but for the associations it evokes of a reality beyond the senses" (5). Mallarmé thought these symbols should not inform, but suggest—"not name things but create their atmosphere," like music (Bowra 9). As a result, he became one of the first poets to think of the poem as an autotelic work of art. But after finding that words as signifiers clung to the narrow meanings of things they signified in the empirical world and remained "impure," Mallarmé went through a crisis in which he stopped writing verse and eventually prefigured the modernists by harboring a radical skepticism about language.

It was during this same period that he discovered ballet. Even though the form had sunk to the dreary, academic dancing at the Paris Opéra, Mallarmé found it a more exemplary symbolist art than either poetry or music. For one thing, its raw material—the human form—could paradoxically transcend the human in content. The ballerina, wrote Mallarmé in "Ballets" (1886), was not a woman dancing, because she was not a woman and she did not dance. The ballerina was an otherworldly creature who wrote poems with her body and who appeared before us as a totally impersonal vessel teeming with abstract, preliterate suggestions. Her "signature" was her ability to summon up elemental, fleeting visions of "a sword, a cup, a flower, etc.," which resonated with indefinite, mysterious meanings (112). Paul Valéry added later that the dancer's world was "an almost inhuman state," discontinuous from nature. He referred to the dancer as an "it," whose gaze turned inward and seemed "to hearken to itself and only to itself, to see nothing as though its eyes were jewels, unknown jewels like those of which Baudelaire speaks" ("Philosophy of Dance" 61).

The doctrine of impersonality is perhaps best understood as a variant of what José Ortega y Gasset described as dehumanization in art; that is, the tendency in modern art to eschew the human in content and purify itself by a conscious deformation of reality. What this means in discourse, according to Roland Barthes, is that "language speaks, not the author; to write, is, through a prerequisite impersonality . . . to reach that point, where only language acts, 'performs' and not 'me.'" Mallarmé's entire poetics, according to Barthes, "consists in suppressing the author in the interests of writing" (115). To Ortega, Mallarmé disappeared in his verse as a "pure, nameless voice." His poetry need not be felt and contains nothing human. "When a woman is mentioned it is 'the woman no one'" (29).

Mallarmé found his model of impersonality, "the woman no one," in the American dancer Loïe Fuller, who submerged her own personality in abstract shapes.[7] An overnight sensation in Paris in 1892, Fuller was hailed as the creator of a new dance art. Unlike Isadora Duncan and Ruth St. Denis, whom she predated, Fuller was less interested in creating steps bound to rhythm than she was in creating a unity where dancing bodies, lights, and costumes captured musical phrases. Her ideas about stagecraft and scenic design were ahead of their time. With long sticks hidden in her sleeves, she manipulated billowing folds of fabric into huge airy configurations. From the play of lights refracting off her fabric, Fuller was able to change herself into surrealistic flowers, birds, butterflies, clouds, and flames. The figure of the dancer was one second revealed, another concealed. She darkened the auditorium, stripped the stage of decor, and hung it with black chenille curtains so that the shapes seemed suspended in air.

The French linked Fuller to the art of her time, placing her dance within the context of art nouveau and symbolism. Toulouse-Lautrec made a poster of her, and sculptor Raoul Larche modeled her into an ormolu lamp with her scarves flying over her head like storm clouds. However, it was the symbolist critics, particularly Mallarmé, who made the greatest fuss. Mallarmé went to see her perform at the Folies-Bergère for the first time in 1893. The critic André Levinson described him "pencilling in his seat, his luminous *aperçus* on the so-called serpentine dances of Loïe Fuller. Since then, the whole world has followed" (Kermode, "Poet and

Symbolist dancer Loïe Fuller. With long sticks hidden in her sleeves, she manipulated billowing folds of fabric into surreal configurations. *Courtesy of the Dance Collection, New York Public Library for Performing Arts, Astor, Lenox, and Tilden Foundations.*

Dancer" 154). Mallarmé called Fuller's performance *sui generis;* it was an "artistic intoxication" and an "industrial achievement." Fuller had the power to create her own ambience out of her dress. This, Mallarmé postulated, would cause an end to the "inanity" of permanent sets, which conflict with choreographic mobility.

> Opaque frames, intrusive cardboard, to the scrapheap! Here, if ever, is atmosphere, that is nothingness, given back to ballet, visions no longer known than scattered, limpid evocation. The pure result will be a liberated stage, at the will of fictions, emanating from the play of a veil with attitude or gesture. (quoted, Kermode, "Poet and Dancer" 155)

He saw her dance as "multiple emanations round a nakedness." Her "statuesque figure strict, upright; *made dead* [emphasis added] by the effort of condensing out of this virtual self-liberation delayed decorative leaps of skies and seas, evenings, scent and foam" (155).

Unlike English and American artists, the French had a tradition of rhapsodizing over dancers: Gautier had his Fanny Elssler; Toulouse-Lautrec, his Jane Avril; Degas, an entire *corps* of anonymous ballerinas. But as Frank Kermode noted: "there is a clear discontinuity between the general admiration for dancers of French poets earlier than Mallarmé and his praise of Fuller. Before, the human and palpable element counted for much. But in the 'new age' of Mallarmé and Yeats, what matters is that the dancer is not a woman; that she is, as Yeats says, 'dead, yet flesh and bone'" ("Poet and Dancer" 157).

The Inadequacy
of Words and Their
"Worn-Out Connotations"

Besides Fuller's impersonality, the shift in poetics starting with Mallarmé and Yeats also indicated a growing sense that, like Mallarmé's criticism of conventional theatrical sets, the surface of language had ceased to be luminous and had grown opaque. The existentialist philosopher Martin Heidegger claimed that language had gone through a "process of deformation and decay" (Bradbury and McFarlane 327). Lawrence would call language a "dumb show" where "all the great words, . . . love, joy, happiness, home, mother, father, husband, . . . were dying from day to day" (*Women in Love* 84; *LCL* 58). All that remained were a few arcane fragments, as Eliot rued in *The Waste Land*, to shore against the ruin of the present. The impossibility of revivifying language was best summed up by another symbolist poet, Hugo von Hofmannsthal (Ruth St. Denis's friend), writing a few years after Mallarmé, when he claimed the future lay with a "language which is no language and that until this language [was] found, the only possibility [was] silence" (Bradbury and McFarlane 324).

Hofmannsthal was probably unaware that Mallarmé had

already found a "language which is no language" in dance. Based on his observations of Fuller and lesser dancers before her, Mallarmé emphasized that dance was a language and an ideal form of communication. Because of her impersonality, the dancer could "suggest things which the written word could only express in several paragraphs of dialogue or descriptive prose. Her poem was written without the writer's tools" ("Ballets" 112). The "illiterate dancer" was an "unwritten body writing" and what she did was more instinctual than what the poet did. Mallarmé exhorted the poet to "humbly place the Flower of your poetic instinct . . . at that sorceress' feet . . . through her always ultimate veil she will give you back your concepts in all their nakedness, and silently inscribe your vision as would a Symbol—which she is" ("Ballets" 115).

The dancer's gestures were symbolic in the same sense that Mallarmé wanted words to be symbolic. To use Philip Wheelwright's instructive definition of a symbol, they were both signifiers "standing for some larger meaning or set of meanings which cannot be given, or not fully given, in perceptual experience itself" (92). But since words obstinately clung still to the things they signified in the outside world, poetry was less spiritual than dance as an incantatory medium for evoking a transcendent reality. To use Wheelwright's schema, words became symbols when they were "repeated and developed by an individual poet and [had] special significance for that person" or when they acquired new life "by being renewed in fresh contexts" when "passed from poet to poet." But a dancer's gestures belonged in Wheelwright's last category, not a literary symbol so much as "an archetype significant for humanity in general" (92).

In his review of Nijinsky's *Le Sacre du printemps,* Jacques Rivière illustrated what Mallarmé meant by the immediacy or primacy of dance writing over literal writing. Rivière compared what Nijinsky had expressed in *Le Sacre* with its articulation in words:

> How different this is from their expression through articulated language . . . by means of this tangible figure we are brought closer to them [words] and put into their presence

in a more immediate manner; we are able to contemplate them before the arrival of language. There is no need of translation; this is not a sign from which the subject must be interpreted. But though our intelligence fails to grasp it, we are there; we are present through our body, and it is the body that understands. A certain predisposition, a certain inner awareness. . . . Each of the dancer's gestures is like a word that I could have said . . . it is thus that we face this extravagant dance with a peculiar barefaced credulity and with a feeling of intimacy that goes beyond words. (122)

Paul Valéry, Mallarmé's disciple, also noticed that what the dancer did was a kind of writing. In "Ballets," Mallarmé had described the dancer: "before taking a step, she invites, with two fingers, a trembling fold of her skirt and simulates a pen-feathered impatience moving toward the Idea." Her legs are a "direct instrument of the Idea" (113–14). Likewise, Valéry had Socrates say of the dancers in "The Dance and the Soul" (1921) that their "hands speak and feet seem to write" (295). His Socrates also realized that the mind alone is incapable of deciphering these strange gestures. "A cold eye would without difficulty see her as demented, this woman strangely uprooted, who wrests herself incessantly away from her own form, whilst her limbs—gone mad—seem to dispute earth and air; . . . and one of her legs takes the place of her head" (310). What the dancer does is the "supreme essay. . . . She turns, and all that is visible detaches itself from her soul" (324).

Valéry also drew out the implications of Mallarmé's linking of poetry and dance through their evocative, "symbolic" language. Both arts, to Valéry, demonstrated "non-usage," like "the not saying 'it is raining'" ("Philosophy of Dance" 62). Poetry, in fact, was to prose as dancing was to walking. Poetry, like movement, was not instrumental; it had no end outside of itself. It was an "action that *derives* from ordinary, useful action, but *breaks away* from it, and finally *opposes* it," according to Valéry (62). For this reason he concluded, as would Yeats and Williams, that dance was a satisfactory emblem of a desirable poetry.

A *poem* . . . is *action,* because a poem exists only at the

moment of being spoken; then it is *in actu.* This act, like the
dance, has no other purpose than to create a state of mind;
it imposes its own laws; it, too, creates a time and measure-
ment of time which are appropriate and essential to it: we
cannot distinguish it from its form of time. To recite poetry
is to enter into a verbal dance. (63)

What the dancer does in space and time, moreover, was a figure
for the poet's creative process. Sometimes the flights of the poet's
mind take him too far from "the ground, from reason, from the
average notion of logic and common sense," leading Valéry to ask:

What is a metaphor if not a kind of pirouette performed by
an idea, enabling us to assemble its diverse names or images?
And what are all the figures we employ, all those instruments,
such as rhyme, inversion, antithesis, if not an exercise of all
the possibilities of language, which removes us from the practical world and shapes, for us too, a private universe, a privileged abode of the intellectual dance? (65)

Besides its evocative power as a symbol, Mallarmé had isolated one more primitive characteristic of dance, which was to have
repercussions on all four modernists. To Mallarmé, dance was a
sacred rite. He called it *"l'incorporation visuelle de l'idée,"* with
"idée" referring to his mystical belief in an Absolute Beauty, incapable of being comprehended rationally. Theater per se he thought
too coarse and music too vague. But dance was the "superlative
theatrical form of poetry" and satisfied his craving for a ritualistic
(as opposed to realistic) theater. Of all the theatrical arts, it "alone
was capable of translating the fleeting, the sudden, even the Idea"
(*Poems, Essays, and Letters* 62). The dance was the "mysterious and
holy interpretation" of universal life and of our inmost being (63).
The movements of the dancer reflected a cosmic dance of the constellations. Echoing Mallarmé's sentiments a few years later, Eliot
would commend Diaghilev's ballets for their simplicity and conclude that what was needed in all art was "a simplification of current life into something rich and strange."[8]

Primitivism:
The Fusing of Dancer and Dance
or Art and Life

Responding to a fragmented, dehumanized, material world where the word had lost much of its magic, the four writers discussed herein regarded dance as a paragon of primitive wholeness; to use Eliot's phrase, dance fused thought and feeling. It represented art in an undissociated and unspecialized form and, like Mallarmé's *Idée,* expressed a truth inaccessible to the intellect alone. Yeats's name for this primitive wholeness was "unity of being" (*E & I* 518). The dancer was a fitting symbol since it was impossible to dissociate or differentiate between the dancer and her dance, form and matter, body and soul, or any other dualities.

The unity of being expressed in a dance represented several different levels of experience. For Yeats and Eliot, unity of being was essentially a mystical idea which signified an escape from the temporal world into some timeless realm. In Yeats's *A Vision,* it is the point in the zodiac where two interlocking gyres touch and form a sphere and the soul escapes from its endless round of reincarnations (Pall 114). In "The Double Vision of Michael Robartes," unity of being is expressed as that "stretched out" moment when linear "time" is "overthrown" and becomes suspended into a Bergsonian duration (*CP* 172). In Eliot's *Four Quartets,* unity of being is figured as a dance at the still point of a turning universe where time and eternity intersect.

For Lawrence and Williams, on the other hand, the unity-of-being scale tipped in favor of the temporal and transient. Specifically, it meant a total moral and ontological acceptance of both the body and the mind. Lawrence associated dance with sex, since they were both mysterious, regenerating rites through which the individual connected to other people as well as the universe. Immediately following love-making with her gamekeeper, Connie Chatterley escapes the confines of his hut to dance naked in the pouring rain, abandoning herself to a wild, ecstatic Dionysian dance "with the eurythmic dance-movements she had learned so long ago in Dresden" (*LCL* 207). Williams, the poet of "no ideas but in things," denied intellectual functions could exist dissociated from sensible material. The unity of being expressed in a dance, therefore, was an apt epistemological model for his theory that "a thing known passes out of the mind into the muscles."

These modernists found support for their views in the writings of anthropologists, critics, and philosophers, all of whom privileged dance for the psychological wholeness and integration it had bestowed on the ancients. Social theorist and sexologist Havelock Ellis, for one, provided an overview in his essay "The Dance of Life" (1923) on how dance functioned in every aspect of ancient life: religion, love, art, work, and morals. Waxing rhapsodically, he concluded that dancing was the "loftiest, the most moving, the most beautiful of the arts, because it is no mere translation or abstraction of life; it is life itself" (254).

To poet and critic Arthur Symons, dance restored our primitive instincts and made us feel whole and undisassociated again. At the same time, it expressed the "modern ideal" in form. In "The World as Ballet" (1898), he insisted that dance had a "preeminence among the more than imitative arts" because it had the intellectual as well as sensuous appeal of a living symbol" (347). According to Symons, "nothing is stated, there is no intrusion of words used for the irrelevant purpose of describing; a world rises before one, the picture lasts only long enough to have been there: and the dancer, with her gesture, all pure symbol, evokes, from her mere beautiful motion, idea, sensation, all that one need ever know of event" (348). Amending Walter Pater's famous dictim, Symons concluded that all the arts should aspire to the condition of dance rather than music.

According to anthropologist Jane Harrison, dance enjoyed a historical primacy over the other arts because of its "inchoateness" and "undifferentiatedness" (171). Her influential book, *Ancient Art and Ritual* (1913), traced the evolution of sacred dance rites into Greek drama, based on Aristotle's statement in the *Poetics* that tragedy originated with the leaders of the Dithyramb, or spring festival associated with the god Dionysus. Art and ritual, Harrison concluded, shared a common root: "it is one and the same impulse that sends a man to church and the theater" (10). Both arose from unsatisfied desire—either from some perception or an emotion that did not find an immediate outlet in practical action (41). In order to ensure their food supply for the coming year, for example, primitive people engaged in rituals. "Ritual consisted not in prayer and praise and sacrifice . . . but in mimetic dancing" (168).

Although his conclusions were vastly different, Nietzsche, in *The Birth of Tragedy,* had also detected a common source underlying Greek religion and drama. According to him, as the Greeks evolved into a secular society, the efficacy of their dancing increased rather than decreased as Harrison supposed. Nietzsche postulated that the ancient Greeks originally gave meaning to their existence by inventing their gods. These gods lived much as humans did; that is, they fought, became jealous, and suffered misery and pain. Greek art and tragedy performed the same function; that is, the Greeks saw in them a mirror that justified human existence. According to Nietzsche, dance was the one artistic creation in which humans did not see their mirror images. Instead, they became that which justified them. Man danced to "feel himself a god. . . . He [was] no longer an artist, he [became] the work of art" (37). Now that all gods were dead, it "[was] only as an aesthetic phenomenon that existence and the world [were] eternally justified" (52, 141).

Paul Valéry, one final advocate of dance's primitive wholeness, would have agreed with a later hero of Nietzsche's, Zarathustra, who danced to ward off his devil, whom he calls "the Spirit of Gravity." The equivalent of this devil in the modern world was what Valéry labeled "the weariness of living" ("Dance and the Soul" 315). Valéry postulated that man did not originally dance to satisfy religious longings. Rather, he always danced for impractical reasons. Because man possessed an abundance of physical energy— more than he needed to satisfy his needs—he discovered that certain movements afforded him a pleasure "equivalent to a kind of intoxication" or ecstasy resulting from an expenditure of that energy. The intoxication afforded by dance was an antidote to the Spirit of Gravity and the ennui resulting from "murderous lucidity, inexorable clarity, . . . the comprehension of life as it really is" (317).

Perhaps man danced, as Nietzsche thought, "to feel himself a god." Perhaps men and women danced for practical reasons to propitiate the gods and ensure the coming of spring and their food supply. Or perhaps they danced for impractical reasons to simply expend some superfluous energy unneeded for survival. For whatever reasons men and women originally danced, primitive dance rituals continued to express some basic nonverbal truths about the human condition. Given the intellectual climate and the desire to find something *real* from the past to authenticate the present, it is not surprising that Yeats, Eliot, Lawrence, and Williams turned to nontheatrical dance rituals for ethical as well as aesthetic reasons. Responding to a world rendered spiritless by positivism, Yeats went digging into the myths and legends of ancient Celts to unite Ireland with its old beliefs. Rebelling against a mechanized, capitalistic society, Lawrence wanted to revive the dark, underground gods of pre-Columbian civilizations like the Aztecs. He journeyed to several Hopi and Zuni pueblos in the Southwest to study their dance rituals first hand. Searching for lost religious values, Eliot wanted to restore liturgical dancing to Christian rituals like the high mass. And Williams, vehemently opposed to the Puritan ban on dancing in the New World, alluded in *Paterson* to several varieties of therapeutic pagan dancing, from the fertility rites of ancient Greece to the death rites (Kinte Kaye) of Native Americans.

Despite critical neglect, the dance did contribute to the character of literary modernism, whether it was through studying ritualized communal dancing or attending theatrical performances. The latter included those of the Ballets Russes, heralded as a new confluence of the arts—Wagner's *Gesamtkunstwerk* realized[9]—as well as the art dances of Loïe Fuller, Ruth St. Denis, and Isadora Duncan, the precursors of a radically new language of movement form.

William Butler Yeats and His Dancers

"I wanted a dance, because where there are no words there is less to spoil."

Yeats,
Prologue to *The Death of Cuchulain* (1934)

Yeats's endless fascination with the dancer in his poetry, prose, and plays, was not an isolated phenomenon. While Mallarmé extolled the virtues of ballet at the Paris Opéra and Loïe Fuller's symbolist art, across the channel, Yeats's friends at the Rhymer's Club—Symons, Wilde, and Ellis—were obsessed with dancers, especially the music hall variety appearing on the stages of the Palace and Alhambra.

But though Yeats's dancer has sources in the decadentism of Mallarmé, Wilde and Symons, she is unique. As Frank Kermode claims, she is "one of Yeats's great reconciling images, containing life-in-death, death-in-life, movement and stillness, action and contemplation, body and soul" (*Romantic Image* 48). The dancer is one of Yeats's antithetical masks and possesses what the poet lacks: a freedom from quotidian time and space and an ability to express concrete images without recourse to language's abstract sign system. Her power as muse, however, is double-edged; she is as capable of leading the poet into an orderly measure as she is into a frenzied, off-balance *danse macabre*. In some poems, the dancer spinning in her "narrow luminous circle" creates a space of desire or lost plenitude, which if recovered results in either psychological, aesthetic, or metaphysical wholeness: in short, unity of being (*Auto* 321). At other times, her violent whirling conveys personal feelings of fragmentation and loss of identity to the poet and cosmically portends an apocalyptic upheaval of civilization.

Dancers spin around Yeats's imagination as early as *The Wanderings of Oisin* (1888) and "The Stolen Child" (1886), where they exist as a band of immortals "of the Danaan kind" or Sidhe, who dance in fairyland under the Celtic moonlight by the seashore. The faeries dance to express their freedom from the shackles of human time, always with a lonely, wistful human there to witness. After 1893, the mythical chorus disappears for a time while Yeats made himself over into a public poet addressing current political topics and a playwright/director of an Irish national theater, which included dance plays. When a single dancer re-emerges in 1912 as a thoroughly modern mortal in "To a Child Dancing in the Wind," she is still dancing on the seashore unfettered by the reality of time. Heaven, not fairyland, is designated the "pre-destined dancing place" (*CP* 159). Starting with "The Double Vision of Michael Robartes" (1919) and throughout Yeats's major period, the dancer and her world become of paramount importance. Dancing is linked to erotic desire and the dancer represents other beautiful women personally and artistically important to the poet (like Maud Gonne). Or dancing is linked to the desire for a mystical, ecstatic wholeness, and the dancers become anonymous souls purging themselves of the "fury and mire of human veins" by dancing on the Emperor's marble tiles in "Byzantium."

Yeats never specifically mentions a desire to be a dancer, but he left a trail of hints that he loved to dance. One of Yeats's alter egos, the narrator of an early short story, "Rosa Alchemica," tells

us he was a good dancer in his youth and "master of many curi-
ous Gaelic steps" (*Mythologies* 286). During his childhood in
Bedford Park, London, Yeats mentions taking dancing lessons
from two sisters of a well-known, but unidentified, Pre-Raphaelite
painter (*Auto* 43–44). During his third American lecture tour in
1914, an older Yeats again takes dancing lessons, this time from the
Petipas sisters, who were boarding his father, John Butler Yeats
(Jeffares, *A New Biography* 201). After smoking Indian hemp with
followers of Saint-Martin, Yeats confesses to an insatiable desire
to dance, which he repressed because he did not know any steps
(*E & I* 281). In commissioning artist T. Sturge Moore to draw
the figure of a dancer on a bookplate for his six-year-old daughter, Yeats must have harbored the hope that Anne would realize
the fantasy for him (Melchiori 58).

As a dramatist, Yeats was profoundly influenced by his exposure to professional dancers. The first—eurythmic-trained, Japanese
dancer Michio Ito—played the Guardian in Yeats's first Noh-
inspired dance play, *At the Hawk's Well* (1916). Seeing Ito dance
at one of Lady Ottoline Morrell's soirees, Yeats wrote: "no stage-
picture made an artificial world; he was able, as he rose from the
floor . . . to recede from us into some more powerful life" (*E & I*
224). The tragic image Ito projected fired Yeats's imagination. As
a Samurai descendant, he represented aristocracy and statuesque
nobility. The way Ito looked in performance—with his face so
immobile that personality was deliberately repressed and idea
enhanced—became a model for the blank stare on the dancers in
Yeats's poetry.

Not long after the first performance of *At the Hawk's Well*,
Ito accepted an offer to bring the play to New York.[1] Yeats found
his replacement eleven years later in Ninette de Valois (née Edris
Stannus) who, as a former member of Diaghilev's Ballets Russes
and the eventual founder of Britain's Royal Ballet, exposed the play-
wright to an entirely different tradition of dance than Ito's. Yeats
arranged for Valois to run a small ballet school at the Abbey Theater
and rewrote *The Only Jealousy of Emer* (called *Fighting the Waves* in

Yeats collaborator Michio Ito, the model for the blank stare on the dancers in Yeats's poetry. *Courtesy of the Dance Collection, New York Public Library for Performing Arts, Astor, Lenox, and Tilden Foundations.*

1929) and *King of the Great Clock Tower* (1934) as dance plays for her to perform in. Following Ito's model, he covered her "most impressive face" with a mask to serve his ideal of anonymity. Valois recalls that her choreography for Yeats was "highly stylized" and that the dances utilized the simplest gestures possible: "with the masks, anything else would have been out of place" (Pinciss 389).

Besides his collaborations with dancers, Yeats helped sponsor Ruth St. Denis's London season and was acquainted with Anna Pavlova and the toast of the French symbolists, Loïe Fuller (Magriel 230). While he never saw Isadora Duncan perform, he received two letters in 1908 from his father, which were glowing, detailed accounts of meeting Duncan in person and seeing her dancing "on the biggest stage in New York—a figure dancing all alone. Several people said: Is it not like watching a kitten playing with itself? We watched her as if we were each of us hidden in ambush" (John Butler Yeats 115–16). The qualities J. B. Yeats depicts in Duncan—her independence and introspection while performing—are projected into W. B. Yeats's composite dancer. The elder Yeats's voyeuristic confession as an observer is especially revealing; it will later creep into the son's observance of the dancer and the longing to forget his solitude and decrepitude by losing himself in the more beautiful, thrilling We of the dance.

Dance also attracted Yeats because of its origins in ancient ritual. Yeats's interest was both patriotic and mystical. He went digging into the myths and legends of the pagan Celts because he felt modern Ireland's unity depended upon the creation of a common mythology. He also felt the values and exploits associated with the old Irish heroes could stay the tide of materialism and scientific rationalism at the turn-of-the-century. The ancient Celts, unpreoccupied with "thoughts of weight and measure," turned their passion for nature instead into a sacred ritual of dancing. "They worshipped nature," according to Yeats, "and the abundance of nature, and had always, as it seems, for a supreme ritual that tumultuous dance among the hills or in the depths of the woods, where unearthly ecstasy fell upon the dancers, until they seemed the gods or the godlike beasts" (*E & I* 178).

"Unearthly ecstasy," like the trancelike, hypnotic state produced in the whirling dervishes of "Byzantium" (who are "Dying into a dance, / An agony of trance" *CP* 248) appealed especially to the occult, mystical Yeats who attended seances and believed in lunar influences. Dance rhythms raised consciousness and transported us beyond the threshold of waking life to "prolong the moment of contemplation, the moment when we are both asleep and awake, . . . the one moment of creation." In this trancelike state, "the mind liberated from the pressure of the will is unfolded in symbols" (*E & I* 159). Rhythm, the narrator asserts in the story "Rosa Alchemica," is the "wheel of Eternity, on which alone the transient and accidental could be broken, and the spirit set free" (*Mythologies* 286).

If the dance served a ritualized function in Yeats, the dancer was one of his primary symbols. Silently spinning on her axis, she is structurally and thematically related to all the gyrating cones, spirals, wheels, Plato's bobbins, spindles, winding stairs, mummies wound in mummy-cloth, and falcons flying in ever-widening circles in Yeats's poetry. The dancer, moreover, has all the salient characteristics of a Yeatsian symbol. For one, her movements are resistant to paraphrase. According to Yeats, "symbolism said things which could not be said so perfectly in any other way." Symbols gave "dumb things voices, and bodiless things bodies" (*E & I* 147). Secondly, her dancing is independent of ethical utility (Kermode, *Romantic Image* 43). According to Yeats, "it is indeed only those things which seem useless or feeble that have any power, and all those things that seem useful or strong—armies, moving wheels, modes of architecture, modes of government, speculations of reason, would have been a little different if some mind long ago had not given itself to some emotion, as a woman gives herself to her lover" (*E & I* 157). More important, the dancer, like other Yeatsian symbols, participates in a higher level of existence. What she signifies is not only untranslatable, her mere evocation has a talismanic effect in a poem. She is a human being moving in ways natural for humans. But in the perfection of her body, she is also a superhuman engaged in highly artificial steps.

For Yeats, she has a divine essence; the dancer is the supreme embodiment of unity of being. In his prose, Yeats explains unity of being through an analogy to the Eucharist. "It is still true that the Deity gives us, according to His promise, not His thoughts or His convictions but His flesh and blood. . . .We only believe in those thoughts which have been conceived not in the brain but in the whole body" (*E & I* 235). In dance, there is no disunity of being because it is impossible to dissociate, split, or distinguish between the dancer's body and soul, the dancer and the dance, or sense and spirit in general. ("All thought becomes an image and the soul / Becomes a body" *CP* 164). Yeats adds that his "Christ" is analogous to Dante's notion of unity of being as a perfectly proportioned female body, Blake's "Imagination," and what the Upanishads call "Self" (*E & I* 518–19).

In another essay, Yeats explains that no split between body and soul had occurred yet in Dante's day, where "men attained to personality in great numbers, or 'Unity of Being'" (*Auto* 291). Nor did the seventeenth-century completely sever thought and feeling, as T. S. Eliot later would concur. John Donne, for example, praises Elizabeth Drury because her "body thought."[2] But on that symbolic morning when, according to Yeats, "Descartes discovered that he could think better in his bed than out of it," body and soul were split into two irreconcilable entities (*Auto* 192). Because she symbolizes unity of being, the dancer functions like a shield to protect the poet from the modern world's "bundle of fragments" (189).

Yeats was also fascinated by the dancer's inward-looking expression. For while the body of a dancer thinks, the face, paradoxically, should not. Most dancers are trained to hide the difficulty and effort of what they do behind an empty, enigmatic smile. The head in ballet, in particular, often watches the rest of the body moving and in so doing suggests the dancer is separate from the performance. From the audience, it looks as if the dancing, like that performed in ancient rituals, has transported the dancer beyond his or her personal ego into a totally impersonal realm. Likewise, the dancer in "The Double Vision of Michael Robartes" looks as though she has put herself into a trance. "For now being dead it seemed / That she of dancing dreamed." She "had outdanced thought. / Body perfection brought" (*CP* 171). The combination of expressionless face and vital body will come to stand for the "life-in-death" and "death-in-life" of "Byzantium."

Yeats read in the dancer's blank gaze an ideal of impersonality, which he tried to achieve in his own art. Like a choreographer shaping individual bodies into something impersonal and formal, Yeats thought that the poet should work on the raw materials of his personal life and "exhaust personal emotion in action or desire so completely that something impersonal, something that has nothing to do with action or desire" results (*Auto* 332). For Yeats, there is nothing wrong with expressing personal emotions in art, but like the dancer's face, they must be rendered "cold" (*Auto* 45).

> A poet writes always of his personal life, in his finest work out of its tragedy, whatever it be; . . . he never speaks directly as to someone at the breakfast table, there is always a phantasmagoria. . . . [H]e is never the bundle of accidents and incoherence that sits down to breakfast; he has been reborn as an idea, something intended, complete. (*E & I* 509)

Eliot, who also extols impersonality in art, thought Yeats achieved greatness only in his mature poetry when he attained this impersonality. "Out of intense and personal experience," according to Eliot, Yeats was "able to express a general truth; retaining all the particularity of experience, to make of it a general symbol" (Cullingford, *Poems* 76). But what Eliot and Yeats mean by impersonality in art are not quite the same things. For Eliot, it is the defining characteristic of an autotelic poem; for Yeats, it is a way of ensuring freedom and creativity in a naturalistic, deterministic universe. Impersonality, in short, is synonymous with the wearing of masks: both the literal, stylized masks of his Noh-inspired dance plays and the figurative use of masks in his poetics and poetry.

Yeats's concept of the mask can only be recapped here: a mask is an image of what we wish to become and the opposite of what we are. "According to this theme," Richard Ellmann says, "a Caesar is buried in every hunchback and a lecher in every saint" (160). According to Yeats, finding "something hard and cold, some articulation of the Image which is the opposite of all that I am in daily life" is a way to guarantee impersonality (*Auto* 274). "I think that all happiness depends on the energy to assume the mask of some other self; that all joyous or creative life is a re-birth as something not oneself, something which has no memory and is created in a moment and perpetually renewed" (306). Only the "man of science, the moralist, the humanitarian, the politician seek to suppress their anti-self [or Mask] till the natural state alone remains" (247).

Yeats was reborn, or at least reanimated, as an artist when the dancer became his antithetical mask. The dancer was the "opposite" of all that he was in "daily life." As Kermode notes, Yeats was incessantly tormented by the choice he had to make between "perfection of the work," which meant leading the isolated, passive existence of an artist or any contemplative man, and "perfection of the life," the active kind of existence he coveted in soldiers and statesmen (*Romantic Image* 23). The labor or cost of perfecting the work turned the poet, even at a young age, into an óld "scarecrow," which is why Yeats always drew the poet as a tragic hero "proving life by the act of withdrawing from it" (25). Because the dance synthesizes doing and thinking, the dancer was one artist-figure who escaped a scarecrow fate. Unlike the poet, who "hammered out headachy fancies with a bent back at an ink-stained table" (23), the dancer in perfecting her work—all those exercises at the barre in front of a mirror—perfected her life in the Yeatsian sense by getting her muscles to think. The more her muscles think, the more beautiful she becomes and the closer she is to attaining unity of being. Self-renunciation, in her case, leads to greater self-realization.

Not only dancers, but *all beautiful women* with perfectly proportioned bodies, like Dante's Beatrice, possess unity of being for Yeats. Obviously, female beauty for him consists of grace and physical élan. In the poem "His Phoenix," included in *The Wild Swans at Coole,* he catalogues beautiful women—both living and legendary—and then compares them to his beloved who, like the phoenix, has the power to repeatedly come alive again in his memory. ("I knew a phoenix in my youth, so let them have their day" *CP* 151.) Among the living "phoenixes," Yeats includes two famous contemporary dancers, the American art dancer Ruth St. Denis, and the Russian ballerina Anna Pavlova. He describes St. Denis having "more charm," while Pavlova, from "nineteen hundred nine or ten . . . had the cry." But compared to the phoenix the speaker knew in his youth, their beauty is not timeless, so the speaker grants them only "their day."

Interestingly, in the original manuscript of "His Phoenix," Jeffares shows that Yeats originally alluded to a third professional dancer, the Canadian Maud Allan (*Commentary* 157). Although

Maud Allan's *The Vision of Salomé* (1908), responsible for unleashing a swarm of dancing *femme fatales.*
Courtesy of the Dance Collection, New York Public Library for Performing Arts, Astor, Lenox, and Tilden Foundations.

her career was shortlived, some contemporary reviewers compared her to Duncan and claimed she was the more beautiful, graceful, and musical of the two (Cherniavsky 120). But Allan is most famous for scandalizing polite society with her solo *The Vision of Salomé*, in which she undulated her torso and arms around a grisly papier-mâché head while dressed in a harness consisting of clusters of heavy pearls and little else. Her Salomé, possibly inspired by Wilde, Moreau, and Richard Strauss's opera, excited Edward VII of England during a private performance, played two hundred engagements at the Palace in London in 1908, and "spawned a horde of imitators" (Jowitt 111).

While Allan is omitted in the final version of "His Phoenix," her persona was to become "almost an obsession in the last years of Yeats's life" (Melchiori 196).[3] In the poems "The Hosting of the Sidhe" and "Nineteen Hundred and Nineteen," Salomé is associated with the Sidhe, or Irish faeries, and the wind. And in *A Vision,* she is assigned to the fifteenth phase along with others who achieve perfect unity of being.

> When I think of the moment before revelation I think of Salomé—she, too, delicately tinted or maybe mahogany dark—dancing before Herod and receiving the Prophet's head in her indifferent hands, and wonder if what seems to us decadence was not in reality the exaltation of the flesh and of civilization perfectly achieved. (273)

Beauty, paradoxically, can be deadly and still remain a symbol of unity of being. Yeats never bothered much with conventional ethics. As we will see, he divests Salomé of her profane trappings so she can bare her soul.

Salomé, the Bible's most famous dancer, was not originally evil. Her story takes up only eleven lines in the Book of Mark (6:17–28), which is conspicuously mute on the nature of Salomé's dancing. Herod (Rome-appointed Tetrarch of Galilee) married his brother Philip's wife, Herodias. Jokanaan, or John the Baptist, publicly decried the marriage as adulterous and called Herodias a whore. Herodias wanted John killed, but Herod "went in awe of John, knowing him to be a good man and holy man; so he kept him in custody" (6:20–21). Salomé, Herodias's daughter, was the instrument of her mother's revenge. Herod was so pleased by her dancing that he offered Salomé anything she desired. She deferred to her mother who told her to demand John's head.

Over the years, artists conflated Salomé and Herodias (throwing in a few sisters as well) into one archetypal *femme fatale* and made her art, or dancing, flagrantly salacious. Dancing before and lusting after the head of John the Baptist, Salomé is the quintessential castrating female who terrorizes male psyches.[4] This was the decadent image Yeats inherited from his friends Oscar Wilde and Arthur Symons. In Wilde's play, for example, Salomé is the epitome of cruelty and desire, a remorseless voluptuary subject only to her own unspeakable appetites. As she coldly confesses to John, *"C'est pour mon propre plaisir que je demande la tete*

[It is for my own pleasure that I demand your head].” Symons, following Wilde's credo that “nothing succeeds like excess,” added some sisters in his poem, “Dance of the Daughters of Herodias” (1897). While they are not innately sadistic like Wilde's heroine, they are the eternal enemy because their beauty is deadly. At the end, the speaker pleads with the sisters not to come too close, or he will suffocate in beauty's surfeit.

Symons's translation of Mallarmé's “Hérodiade” also had a hand in shaping Yeats's composite image of the dancer. The poem left such a deep and lasting impression on Yeats that he recalled twenty-five years later the day Symons read it to him in the flat they shared at Fountain Court. The subject of Mallarmé's poem is not so much cruel as she is a narcissistic “inviolate reptile” in love with her own virginity.

> The horror of my virginity
> Delights me, and I would envelop me
> In the terror of my tresses, that, by night,
> Inviolate reptile, I might feel the white
> And glimmering radiance of thy frozen fire,
> Thou that art chaste and diest of desire,
>
> . . . .
>
> And all about me lives but in mine own
> Image, the idolatrous mirror of my pride,
> Mirroring this Hérodiade diamond-eyed.
>
> (*Auto* 321)

After Yeats quotes the above lines from “Hérodiade” in his essay “The Tragic Generation,” he makes a revealing connection between Mallarmé's dancer and his own art.

> Yet I am certain that there was something in myself compelling me to attempt creation of an art as separate from everything heterogeneous and casual, from all character and circumstance, as some Hérodiade of our theatre, dancing seemingly alone in her narrow moving luminous circle. (321)

Yeats's feelings about his role as an artist are reflected in his image of the dancer. In some poems, such as "Nineteen Hundred and Nineteen," she resembles the romantic/decadent image of the woman-as-destroyer, and the poet's desire for her is an intermingling of eros and thanatos, or love and death. Out of her spinning, she weaves a violent web which paralyzes anyone who gazes at her. Whenever this occurs, Yeats identifies with John the Baptist's perspective, for Yeats felt the poet had a priestly mission. If John was castrated to honor his God, the artist was likewise forced to sacrifice his life for his art. As in Symons's poem, too much beauty is overwhelming and leaves Yeats feeling like an "old scarecrow" at a young age—isolated and estranged from others.

The dancer's beauty, however, is not always threatening. As the above passage on Mallarmé's "Hérodiade" makes clear, Yeats often identifies with Salomé rather than her sacrificial victim. His desire was to create an aristocratic art to express an essentially tragic view of life, "to create for myself an unpopular theater and an audience like a secret society where admission is by favour and never to many" (quoted, Archibald 116). "Like some Hérodiade of our theater," Yeats dons the impersonal, solipsistic mask of the dancer, because like her, his art is aloof and virginal in eschewing all contact with reality.

In identifying with his female dancer, Yeats also wears the androgynous mask of an artist. As such, he is like the Hindu god, the dancing Shiva, who is both male spirit and female matter and another manifestation of unity of being.[5] Yeats was familiar with Ananda Coomarswamy's *The Dance of Shiva* (1917) and knew that Shiva is also Natraj, the lord of the dancers. In rhythmic motion, he both destroys and creates the world. Salomé, too, both destroys and creates. Like Helen of Troy, her beauty caused one civilization to topple and another to rise in its wake. Most important, the dancing Shiva, like the artist and his symbol of art, is beyond such antitheses as male/female, sacred/profane, time/eternity, stillness/movement, love/hate and beauty/death. The dancer has always been, as Yeats says of the mask in general, "part of our being, and yet of our being but as water with fire, a noise with silence" (*Mythologies* 332).

The Dance of the "Ever-Living Ones" under the Celtic Twilight: 1889–93

Dancing in the early poetry is largely the result of Yeats's efforts to create a universal Irish mythology. Only the faeries (immortals or ever-living ones, as they are variously called) outdance time in the poetic landscape. Their collective dancing is a ritualized expression of immortality, characterized by endless youth, joy, passion, and erotic love. Dance, moreover, always appears within a cluster of other central Yeatsian symbols, which remain more or less consistent throughout the collected poems. The faeries, for example, always dance under the moonlight, either by the seashore or on a rocky mountaintop. Later, in *The Wind among the Reeds* (1899), dance becomes associated with a third natural element, the "luminous wind," whose blowing becomes increasingly significant as a personal symbol. (Fire and dance are conflated later in the poetry when dance becomes purgatorial, as in "Byzantium.") Although the moon eventually evolves into the exceedingly complex symbolism of *A Vision,* it here retains its traditional associations with the imagination and creativity.

Richard Ellmann categorizes dance in the early poems as a "cooperative" symbol, which he defines as auxiliary to or supportive of a main symbol, such as the rose (63). Dance for Ellmann "represents both the state of fairyland and the state of blessedness, realms not identical but akin" (79). While its meaning in such poems as "Who Goes with Fergus" or "The Man Who Dreamed of Fairyland" might be categorized under this rubric, in others like *The Wanderings of Oisin,* "The Stolen Child," and "The

Hosting of the Sidhe," the dance constitutes a more complex and threatening symbol.

In *Oisin*, for example, the poet is equivocal about the "rushing" choral dance of the faeries (*CP* 375–86). The poem, considered Yeats's first major work, taps the universal myth of a mortal's abduction by a god to the other world. The faery goddess Niamh, daughter of the Celtic god of love, Aengus, picks Oisin, son of the mighty Irish warrior Finn, to be her lover because she is enamored with Oisin's name. When Oisin sees Niamh, her desire is reciprocated. Together they ride away on horseback from the mortal world to three enchanted islands—the Isles of Dancing, Victory, and Forgetfulness—their sojourn on each lasting one hundred years. Oisin is finally overcome by his yearning to return to Ireland and his Fenian friends, Bran, Sceolan, and Lomair:

> With whom I hurled the hurrying spear,
> And heard the foemen's buckle's rattle,
> And broke the heaving ranks of battle!
>
> (122–24)

After returning, however, Oisin dispels Niamh's magical faery spell by touching the earth and finds himself a "creeping old man, full of sleep, with the spittle on his beard never dry" and his pagan friends long "accurst and dead," burning in hell (book 3 line 92). Events unfold in flashback; the poem begins three-hundred-years after Oisin's abduction, with Ireland Christian and in the hands of a stern, censorious Saint Patrick, who interrogates Oisin about the latter's lengthy "dalliance with a demon thing."

Occurring solely in book 1, dancing in *Oisin* symbolizes both immortality and erotic love. The immortals on the Isle of Dance, "youths, mighty of limb" and "merry as birds," are always evoked in the throes of a "wild and sudden dance" in which they "mock at Death and Time with glances / And wavering arms and wandering glances" (lines 274–75). The island itself is a prelapsarian garden where crimson damask roses bloom in the "sloping green De Danaan sod" by a glimmering, pearl-pale, dove-gray sea.

Here "there is nor law nor rule, / Nor have hands held a weary tool; / And here there is nor change nor Death, / But only kind and merry breath" (lines 282–85). As the faeries sing to Oisin,

> care cannot trouble the least of our days
> Or the softness of youth be gone from our faces,
> Or love's first tenderness die in our gaze.
>
> (lines 409–11)

Contrary to what the faeries sing, Niamh's home on the Isle of Dance is clouded with ambivalence. For one thing, it cannot be the land of all hearts' desires or Niamh would not have sought love in the human world. As Marianne Moore would say, there seems to be a real toad lurking somewhere in this imaginary garden: that is, the desirability of eternal life, love, changelessness, and a world free of conflict. Oisin, for instance, is taken to a hall where the god of love, Aengus,

> dreams, from sun to sun,
> A Druid dream of the end of days
> When the stars are to wane and the world be done.
>
> (lines 218–20)

The content of his dream, annihilation of the world, is not something one would normally associate with fairyland. Even the dancers eagerly anticipate a finale to the cosmic dance as they sing to Oisin:

> "the love-dew dims our eyes till the day
> When God shall come from the sea with a sigh
> And bid the stars drop down from the sky,
> And the moon like a pale rose wither away."
>
> (lines 424–27)

Presumably, when the stars and moon are annihilated and the cosmic dance ceases, the faery dance will as well. This dance occupies the middle links on the Great Chain of Being, half way between St. Patrick's God, or prime mover, and the human/natural world's dance to the changing of the seasons, to birth and decay. The paradox is that the faeries' dance transcends nature but only lasts as long as nature does.

There is also a lot of anxious talk about sorrow and sadness in fairyland. Oisin tells St. Patrick that when he was given a harp and bid to sing a song of "human joy," a "sorrow wrapped each merry face," and they wept until some "tearful boy" grasped his harp and threw it away.

> And each one said, with a long, long, sigh,
> "O saddest harp in all the world,
> Sleep there till the moon and the stars die!"
>
> (lines 244–46)

Later in his speech, Aengus says "things grown sad are wicked" and repeatedly states what a great quality joy is:

> And if joy were not on the earth,
> There were an end of change and birth,
> And Earth and Heaven and Hell would die.
>
> (lines 270–72)

Apparently the god of love has already forgotten that he dreamed or desired the above would happen in lines 219–20. Immediately following his speech, Oisin and the faeries "in a wild and sudden dance / . . . mocked at Time and Fate and Chance" (lines 290–91). According to Hazard Adams, their dancing is either a "symbolic projection" into Aengus's "Druid dream of the end of days," some kind of "anti-time," or a "ritual forgetting of impending annihilation" (31). At this point the poet seems either unable or unwilling to resolve the ambiguity.

In a shorter lyric, "The Stolen Child" (*CP* 18–19), a chorus of faeries also,

> . . . foot it all the night,
> Weaving olden dances,
> Mingling hands and mingling glances.
>
> (lines 16–18)

Dance is directly associated with the moon or creative principle, as the faeries' dance begins when a "wave of moonlight . . . glosses / The dim grey sands with light" and ends when the moon has "taken flight." Like *Oisin,* the poem is about the abduction of a mortal—this time an innocent child—into fairyland. This world is also both inviting and threatening. The repeated siren call of the faery chorus (which modulates rhythmically from the rest of the stanza) beckons the child to join in the dance and escape "From a world more full of weeping than he can understand" (line 53). In fact, the first three stanzas build into a seductive image of Arcadia inhabited by carefree, mischievous nymphs and satyrs who address the child as "the solemn-eyed." But the fourth and final stanza dramatically changes point of view; the warm, familiar human world with its images of domesticity ("the kettle on the hob," "the brown mice" bobbing "round the oatmeal chest") is more substantial than the romantic but cold faery landscape (lines 46–49).

The possible threat to the human world of ecstatic "wavering arms and glances" among the faery hordes is made more explicit in "The Hosting of the Sidhe," the first poem in *The Wind among the Reeds* (1899) (*CP* 55).[6] Once again, faeries are featured as an ambiguous bunch. In one line they beckon: "Empty your heart of its mortal dream." A few lines down they threaten:

> And if any gaze on our rushing band,
> We come between him and the deed of his hand,
> We come between him and the hope of his heart.
>
> (lines 10–12)

In this poem, Yeats collapses all of ancient Ireland into the galloping members of the supernatural host. Caoilte, for example, was one of Finn's mighty warriors whom Oisin yearned to return to in the mortal world. Niamh, Oisin's faery lover, also reappears, seducing again with the repeated, incantatory phrase: "Away, come away." Their "breasts are heaving," their "eyes are aglow," their "hair unbound," the Sidhe seem to heighten or intensify erotic desire, only to frustrate it once it is aroused.

The link between erotic desire and dance is strengthened here. Although the word "dance" never appears, there is a verbal dance in the whirl of movement and energy generated by participles (e.g., "rushing," "tossing," "heaving," "burning," "calling," "Hosting") and in the frenzied onslaught of a repetitive, trancelike rhythm where stressed and unstressed syllables are sharply distinguished, and the caesuras dividing parallel, syntactical utterances are the only times the speaker is allowed to come up for air out of the whirlwind (lines 6–9).

Yeats appended a lengthy gloss to the poem which explicitly associates the Sidhe with Salomé and the dance:

> Sidhe is also Gaelic for wind, and certainly the Sidhe have much to do with the wind. They journey in whirling wind, the winds that were called the dance of the daughters of Herodias in the Middle Ages, Herodias doubtless taking the place of some old goddess. When country people see the leaves whirling on the road they bless themselves, because they believe the Sidhe to be passing by. (*CP* 454)

According to Harold Bloom, the main source for this wind (which becomes increasingly troublesome to the poet) is Shelley's winds of "destruction-creation, which blow all through his poetry" but especially in his "Ode to the West Wind" (124). Salomé, the daughter of Herodias, is a variation of the romantic/decadent *femme fatale*. But it was Yeats's unique achievement to conflate the Sidhe, wind, and Salomé into an apocalyptic *danse macabre*. To be "touched" by the faeries in the vortex of a whirlwind is a symbol of poetic inspiration. There's a fine line, however, between inspiration and madness. Because they "come between him and the deed of his hand," their dance thwarts the artistic process. The same cluster of symbols in the poem "Nineteen Hundred and Nineteen" constitutes a similar frenzied vision of chaos and madness. The muse, like Orpheus's Maenads, can literally leave the poet feeling fragmented, disoriented—the mind disassociated from the heart—as she severs his head and serves it to him on a silver platter.

The Dance by a Female Soloist: 1912–19

The faery hordes and Celtic heroes vanish, and in their place emerges a real, solitary female dancer who is foregrounded in the symbolic landscape. With her grace, poise, and physical presence, the dancer is a type of feminine beauty as "His Phoenix," written during this period, makes clear. She is also young, innocent, and virginal and dances "seemingly alone" in a self-contained, narrow "luminous circle." Like the immortals' dance in the previous poems, her movements constitute a momentary freedom from time and space.

Yeats's first "modern" dancer appears in "To a Child Dancing in the Wind," written in 1912. She is supposedly Maud Gonne's daughter, Iseult, who like her mother rejected Yeats's hand in marriage. The reader hardly needs a biographical gloss to feel the speaker's longing for the dancer and the quality she represents:

> Dance there upon the shore;
> What need have you to care
> For wind or water's roar?
> And tumble out your hair
> That the salt drops have wet;
> Being young you have not known
> The fool's triumph, nor yet
> Love lost as soon as won,

Nor the best labourer dead

And all the sheaves to bind.
What need have you to dread
The monstrous crying of wind?

(*CP* 122)

Her dance of innocence contrasts with the speaker's song of experience, figured in the "monstrous crying" of the Salomé/Sidhe wind. Unterecker calls the poem "brilliantly versified," especially in the "astonishing change of pace achieved by the suddenly introduced slow rhythm of the last line" (*Reader's Guide to Yeats* 126). The stately, elegant dancelike rhythm mirrors the theme. At this point in his career, the poet was learning from the dance how to break a line in simple, graceful cadences close to everyday speech.

The subject of "Her Courage," while not a dancer, anticipates a freedom from time and space, imagined as heaven or the "pre-destined dancing" place (*CP* 159). Comprising the elegy "Upon a Dying Lady," the poem was one of seven short lyrics written between 1912 and 1914, which were addressed to Mabel Beardsley, artist Aubrey's sister (Jeffares, *Commentary* 163). Yeats visited her regularly during the long months when she was dying of cancer. It is appropriate that Mabel's soul will fly to a dancing place, or state, since this "Beauty" is portrayed with the same "old distinguished grace," self-sufficiency, and innocence that Yeats's dancers possess. For even though Mabel was in her early forties when she died, Yeats has her "playing like a child" with dolls in the poem. He draws her as a surrogate artist, and her childlike attachment to images, like Yeats's attachment to his dancers, is her way of imposing shape on the imminent reality of death. Later, the "pre-destined dancing place," the state in which the soul escapes the wheel of endless becoming, or reincarnation, becomes the central image of "Byzantium." Here, the poet's image of an afterlife is embryonic, and he concedes the limited power of his verse to stay death: "I have no speech but symbol, the pagan speech I made / Amid the dreams of youth" (lines 2–3).

Another "girl at play," the dancer in "The Double Vision of Michael Robartes" (written in 1919 and included as the last poem in *The Wild Swans at Coole*), takes on pluri-significance and is a harbinger of the great, complex dance poems to come in the next ten years (*CP* 170–72). The image's former resonances, however, are retained: the dancing occurs in a dream state, or vision, that the speaker, Michael Robartes, experiences on the "grey rock of Cashel."[7] Dancing is conjoined to the earth rather than wind and water, but still transpires under the "moon's light." The dancing girl, along with the immobile images of Sphinx and Buddha that flank her in Robartes's vision, transcend time and space.

> In contemplation had those three so wrought
> Upon a moment, and so stretched it out
> That they, time overthrown,
> Were dead yet flesh and bone.
>
> (lines 45–48)

Like her faery predecessors, Robartes's dream dancer is quite physical and erotic. She flings into his "meat / A crazy juice that makes the pulses beat," causing him to feel "undone / By Homer's Paragon" (lines 53–54, 55–56). Her beauty, in other words, is powerful enough to bring the walls of civilization tumbling down like that of her mythic counterpart Helen of Troy, who "never gave the burning town a thought" (line 57).

Yet the dancer also reveals changes occurring in the poet and his world in the second decade of the century. Yeats had begun work on *A Vision*, his attempt to create a theory of personality and history based on the twenty-eight phases of the moon. The dancer makes her debut in this poem as the chief representative of the antithetical fifteenth phase, when the moon is at its fullest. This phase symbolizes complete beauty, imagination, and self-realization. It is also a nonhuman or supernatural phase, like its opposite, the objective first phase when the moon is dark. Yeats thought unity of being was possible only in those phases closest to the fifteenth. The dancer in Robartes's vision, supernatural and ideal creature that she is, achieves the humanly impossible: the total harmony of body and soul ("So she had outdanced thought. / Body perfection bought," lines 39–40).

Her presence in this poem also signals an apocalyptic upheaval of civilization. In *A Vision,* as noted, she dances at the moment before revelation, an event which occurs every two thousand years, when one civilization is violently overthrown by its opposite. After Dublin's Easter Uprising in 1916, which lead to the brutal executions of his friends at the hands of the British, and the bloody aftermath of the Civil War throughout Ireland, Yeats was convinced the demise of Western, Judeo-Christian civilization was imminent. Out of this destruction—the "frenzy of our western seas"—the dancer's spinning heralds the dawn of a new age.

The dancer, along with the oriental figures of Sphinx and Buddha, suggests the kind of new age the poet was expecting. Yeats often found in Eastern thought and religion what he found lacking in the West. As he had turned to the Japanese Noh for his dance plays, Yeats drew on his knowledge of Hindu aesthetics to shape the dancer in Robartes's vision. Hinduism never rent the body and soul in two like the Judeo-Christian tradition; the spiritual and sexual do not exist in dichotomous relation. Indian dance is a fusion of religion and art because it originated in the god Shiva's dance of ultimate reality. The Hindu concept of *murti,* which signifies that the deity is embodied in the human body, sanctions human dancing and makes it divine. The dancer in Robartes's vision, moreover, has the same serene, blank stare as the dancing god, Shiva. "For now being dead it seemed / That she of dancing dreamed" (lines 23–24). The Hindu god's face is "neither sorrowful nor joyous, but is the visage of the Unmoved Mover, beyond yet present within, the world's bliss and pain" (Campbell 129). Juxtaposed to Shiva's twisted torso and undulating arms, his head is balanced and still: a synecdoche for the stillness at the center of a fluctuating, illusory universe.[8]

Dancing in History, Heaven, and Purgatory: 1921–30

The dancer's dragon of abstract thought that Robartes tries to slay in "Michael Robartes and the Dancer" (which follows "Double Vision" in *The Collected Poems*, 175–76) rears its ugly head again as the "dragon of air" (line 51) that violently whirls around Loïe Fuller's Chinese (actually Japanese) dancers on "its own furious path" (line 53) in "Nineteen Hundred and Nineteen" (*CP* 206–10).

> When Loïe Fuller's Chinese dancers enwound
> A shining web, a floating ribbon of cloth,
> It seemed that a dragon of air
> Had fallen among dancers. . . .
>
> (lines 49–52)

It is also a dragon of time. Days now, the poet tells us,

> . . . are dragon-ridden, the nightmare
> Rides upon sleep: a drunken soldiery
> Can leave the mother, murdered at her door,
> To crawl in her own blood, and go scot-free. . . .
>
> (lines 25–28)

The poem was a response to the atrocities committed by the Black and Tans, the English troops sent to Ireland to squash the Irish Republican Army. More generally, "Nineteen Hundred and Nineteen" is in the same category as T. S. Eliot's *The Waste Land*, D. H. Lawrence's *Women in Love*, Virginia Woolf's *Mrs. Dalloway*, and other texts reflecting the disillusionment experienced in the wake of World War I. Before the war, we "dreamed to mend / Whatever mischief seemed / To afflict mankind" (lines 84–86). Now the poet realizes

> . . . no work can stand,
> Whether health, wealth or peace of mind were spent

. . . .
No honour leave its mighty monument. . . .

(lines 35–38)

For the "dragon of air" is also the "levelling wind" that obliterates everything—love, youth, individual life, and entire civilizations (line 97). Like Loïe Fuller's elusive dance, all works of art and intellect exist at the vanishing point—from "Phidias' famous ivories," emblems of Athenian civilization broken "in bits," to laws that just a few years ago were "indifferent to blame or praise, / To bribe or threat" (lines 10–11). The poet concludes: "Man is in love and loves what vanishes, / What more is there to say?" (lines 42–43).

Even in the face of mutability, Yeats seems intent on investigating the shapes of change. But he has done so in a structure in many ways analogous to a Loïe Fuller symbolist dance. If "All men are dancers," Yeats is the invisible choreographer calling the tune to the "barbarous clangour of a gong" (lines 57, 58). When Fuller manipulated billowing folds of silk fabric with hidden wands under her sleeves while illuminated from above and below on a transparent platform, the result was a series of *trompe l'oeil* metamorphoses in which her figure became hidden in shapes that actually went swelling, spiraling, and subsiding through space. The rush of kaleidoscopic, curvilinear images she created from nature (such as clouds, flowers, or flames) registered quick emotional changes (such as delight, mourning, or anger). They could be playful one instant, macabre the next. Her images were as insubstantial as dreams and as eerie as hallucinations. She became, in Mallarmé's words, "the visual embodiment of an idea." And because the human form was camouflaged by fabrics, colors, and lights, Fuller's impersonality rendered dance "modern."

The absence of one identifiable speaker in "Nineteen Hundred and Nineteen"—the voice of the poet "lost amid the labyrinth" he has made of the poem (line 70)—is analogous to the absence of human form buried within abstract shapes. Where

Fuller imaginatively transformed the human into visual images, Yeats worked on verbal ones, transforming them, like Fuller, into a phantasmagoria of abrupt emotional turns and tone shifts. David B. McWhirter has pointed out the diversity of moods in the poem, which swing from formal regret, quiet meditation, and scathing irony to prophetic fury (45–46). In addition, the most hetero-geneous images are yoked together without logical transitions: a natural image will suddenly metamorphose into a hallucinatory or supernatural one, like Loïe Fuller's Chinese dancers evolving into the witchlike daughters of Herodias in the climatic *danse macabre*. Herodias's daughters had magically materialized out of the gar-landed, ghostly riders of the wind, or Sidhe, brought back from the earlier poem, "The Hosting of the Sidhe," and they in turn dissolve into the image of Lady Kyteler (the only witch ever tried in medieval Ireland) who lusted after her incubus, "that insolent fiend Robert Artisson," or Robin, son of Art (line 128).

The overwhelming sense of violence the poet perceived in his world is reflected in a cluster of "unmanning" imagery in the final section's allusion to Herodias's daughters and the severed head:

> . . . evil gathers head:
> Herodias' daughters have returned again,
> A sudden blast of dusty wind and after
> Thunder of feet, tumult of images,
> Their purpose in the labyrinth of the wind;
> And should some crazy hand dare touch a daughter
> All turn with amorous cries, or angry cries,
> According to the wind, for all are blind.
>
> (lines 117–24)

The dancers decapitate the men who love them by luring them into the whirlwind's center: "evil gathers head," Yeats puns. The poem ends with "love-lorn" Lady Kyteler offering dismembered peacocks (a symbol for Yeats of the annunciation) and "combs of her cocks" (another image of "unmanning") to her demon lover (line 130).

While not mutilated, other images of isolated body parts seem grotesque when used as synecdoches for the human condition. The phrase "All teeth were drawn" in line 17 (referring to mankind's relative well-being before the war) is linked to "weasels fighting in a hole" in line 32, which is further linked to the four short lines comprising section 4:

> We, who seven years ago
> Talked of honour and of truth,
> Shriek with pleasure if we show
> The weasel's twist, the weasel's tooth.
>
> (lines 89–92)

The cluster of images describing humanity as a toothy, sadistic, shrieking rodent is finally dissolved in the "shrieking wind," which blows everywhere in the poem, leaving behind a trail of destruction. McWhirter calls these image patterns "shape-shifters," or verbal devices "that seem utterly changed each time they reappear" (49), much like Fuller's *trompe l'oeil* creations.

Besides the eerie, enigmatic imagery, "Nineteen Hundred and Nineteen" resembles a symbolist dance in a still more general sense. Its entire structure is mirrored in the image of Fuller's whirling Japanese dancers swallowed up and deconstructed by a "dragon of air." According to J. Hillis Miller, the shape of the poem is a "whirlwind," "maze," or "labyrinth of the wind," which constantly whirls around a missing center (*Linguistic Moment* 325). The missing center is a metaphor for the sense of post–World War I loss mentioned earlier, a malaise experienced by the poet and other writers of his generation ("Things fall apart; the centre cannot hold," *CP* 187). The poem's circularity is reinforced in such imagery as the "shining web" (line 50), the "circle of the moon" (line 3) and the repeated echoing of words like "round," "enwound" and "wearied running round and round in their courses" (line 116). The English "guardsmen's drowsy chargers" (line 24) go around and become the last section's apparitional horsemen, just as Loïe Fuller's dancers spin around and become

Herodias's daughters. Increasingly in the later poetry, Yeats saw life as movement and history as a dance of never-ending cycles.

The first seven stanzas of "Among School Children," like "Nineteen Hundred and Nineteen," deal with the ravages of chronological time (*CP* 215–17). But the idea is brought home more forcibly by the addition of a clearly recognizable, first-person speaker waxing bitterly about his decrepit old age.[9] In his present context, as a "sixty-year-old smiling public man" inspecting a convent classroom (line 8), he is painfully self-conscious about appearing to be an "old scarecrow" in the children's eyes (line 32). He also seems troubled and saddened whenever his thoughts drift to the past. The children remind him of his beloved, Maud Gonne, when she was young and beautiful and of the "Ledaean kind" (line 29), like Helen of Troy. Where she used to have "that colour upon cheek" and "hair" as the children before him (line 22), she is now "hollow of cheek" and devoid of color, as if she coldly "drank the wind / And took a mess of shadows" to eat (lines 27–28). The speaker even tries recasting her present image in his mind by comparing it to a Botticelli painting; "Did Quattrocento finger fashion it?" he wonders (line 26). But an emaciated, spectral image is all that remains of her former glory. Beauty, therefore, is "born of its own despair" because it is doomed to vanish (line 59). The children also remind him of his former relationship with Maud. In the past, she had told him a "tale" about "a harsh reproof, or trivial event" (line 11), which had the power to bring them into harmony: their "two natures blent / Into a sphere from youthful sympathy" (lines 13–14). Now all the poet has are "tales" to tell as a way of coping with her absence. The loss of beauty and love lead him into deeper, depressing musings on the betrayal of maternal love in the fifth stanza. If the poet's mother were alive and could see the disfigured shape of her son "With sixty or more winters on its head" (line 38), would she not feel cheated by "the pang of his birth, / Or the uncertainty of his setting forth?" (lines 39–40). Nor is "blear-eyed wisdom" (line 60) an adequate compensation for a "bruised" body (line 58). By the time the greatest philosophers—Plato, Aristotle, Pythagoras—penetrated the mysteries of nature, nature had turned them into "Old clothes upon old sticks to scare a bird" (line 48).

Then in the final stanza, something miraculous happens. The speaker is no longer aware of himself as old, misshapened, and unloved. His earlier self-mocking ironic tone changes into an exalted, triumphant one.

> Labour is blossoming or dancing where
> The body is not bruised to pleasure soul,
> Nor beauty born out of its own despair,
> Nor blear-eyed wisdom out of midnight oil.
> O chestnut tree, great rooted blossomer,
> Are you the leaf, the blossom or the bole?
> O body swayed to music, O brightening glance,
> How can we know the dancer from the dance?
>
> (lines 57–64)

How did Yeats arrive at this sudden affirmative leap of hopefulness? The typical New Critical explanation begins with a discussion of unity of being symbolized by the "leaf, blossom and bole" of the chestnut tree and the indivisibility of the dancer and dance.[10] The latter, in particular, is an emblem for a spiritual truth which, like Platonic forms, Yeats felt could not be known apart from its concrete revelation. This interpretation cites one of Yeats's last letters in which he wrote:

> Man can embody the truth but he cannot know it. . . . The abstract is not life and everywhere draws out its contradictions. You can refute Hegel, but not the Saint or the Song of Sixpence. (*Letters* 922)

The New Critical strategy is then to work backwards, culling out image patterns from the previous seven stanzas that support unity of being. Unterecker, for example, isolates a series of parallel trinities in the poem: three kinds of worshippers of images (mother, nun, and lover); three kinds of feelings for images (passion, piety, and affection); three philosophers (Plato, Aristotle, and Pythagoras); three parts of a tree (leaf, blossom, and bole); and finally the undis-associated trinity of dance, dancer, and music (190). Archibald adds to the list: three locations in the poem (schoolroom, mind (which includes memories, speculations, and imagination), and a visionary realm beyond space and time); three Yeatses (son, lover, and pub-lic man/artist); three Maud Gonnes (child, beloved, and elderly, gaunt woman); and three states of reality (art, nature, and the ideal) (222–23). These trinities, which appear to be antinomies, really func-tion as a unity like the Christian God.

Paul de Man, in his *Allegories of Reading,* claims the final two lines disrupt or deconstruct the New Critical reading of underly-ing continuity in the poem. According to him, the concluding lines are generally read as a rhetorical question that asserts the impos-sibility of knowing the dancer through the dance. In asking a rhetorical question, Yeats is denying any discrepancy between sign and referent or signifier and signified.[11] "It is equally possible," de Man writes, "to read the last line literally rather than figuratively, as asking with some urgency the question, . . . how can we pos-sibly make the distinctions that would shelter us from the error of identifying what cannot be identified? . . . The figural reading, which assumes the question to be rhetorical, is perhaps naive, whereas the literal reading leads to greater complication of theme and statement" (11). The critic cannot separate the literal, gram-matical meaning of the question—the form of the utterance—from its rhetorical performance, since in this poem the two readings can-cel each other out. Unity of being, despite the numerous image patterns in the poem which support it, is subverted by the language of the poem, which according to DeMan, asserts the discontinu-ity between "signifier and signified."

Yeats's ideas about unity of personality, especially his theory of the Mask, provide yet another reading of the final lines in "Among School Children." "All unity is from the Mask," Yeats wrote, which is a "form created by passion to unite us with our-selves" (*A Vision* 82). The antithetical mask is defined as the oppo-site of what we are and "the image of what we wish to become, or of that to which we give our reverence" (83). A man or woman's particular mask depends on which of the moon's twenty-eight phases he or she was born under. Yeats is purposely vague about naming his own mask, but what he says about Dante is self-revealing, since they both belong to phase seventeen. The problem for a man of this phase is fragmentation and lack of coherence in the self. The mask specific to him is "simplification through intensity" (142). By intensifying his energy, a seventeenth-phase man will become orderly and simple as opposed to complex and fragmented. The problem, however, is that the "Body of Fate," which is characterized by loss, "works to make impossible simplification through intensity":

> The being, through the intellect, selects some object of desire for a representation of the Mask as Image, some woman perhaps, and the Body of Fate snatches away the object. Then the intellect (Creative Mind), which is [best described] as imagination, must substitute some new image of desire . . . and relate that which is lost. (142)

Dante, for example, first finds Beatrice as an object of desire, loses her, and then finds her again as an ideal of beauty and justice. "Dante suffering injustice and the loss of Beatrice, found divine justice and the heavenly Beatrice" (144).

The heavenly Beatrice is to Dante what the dancer is to Yeats. In finding their antithetical masks, both poets attain unity of personality or being. In Freudian terms, Yeats sublimated for lost romantic and maternal love evoked in the first seven stanzas of the poem by creating a substitute image of art. According to David Lynch, the dancer is a signifier of desire; that is, Yeats's obsession with the image is a result of a deferred and displaced desire for Maud Gonne and the withheld (and harder to document) desire for his mother, Susan Yeats.[12] Yeats's dancer, however, is a significant departure from Dante's mask in Beatrice. With her "brightening glance," the former restores the passion and intensity of a sexual entanglement and offers unqualified acceptance and spiritual nourishment like a mother. No one is excluded from her dance on account of age, intellect, or disfigurement. The poet's ecstatic reunion with his mask allows him to unburden himself of paralyzing self-consciousness and to feel vital and immersed in an unknowable, collective Otherness. Loosing himself in the beat of the rhythm, he finds a momentary beatitude. According to Yeats, this loosing of oneself in a passionate, collective "We" is what Synge meant when he wrote:

> In a moment I was swept away in a whirlwind of notes. My breath and my thoughts and every impulse of my body became a form of dance, till I could not distinguish between the instrument or the rhythm and my own person or consciousness. . . . For a while it seemed an excitement that was filled with joy; then it grew into an ecstasy where all existence was lost in the vortex of movement. I could not think that there had been a life beyond the whirling of the dance. (*E & I* 332)

In "Nineteen Hundred and Nineteen," the "place" where "labour is blossoming or dancing" (line 57) is a far cry from Niamh's Isle of Dancing in *Oisin*, a prelapsarian garden where time is barred. Here, trees get diseased and withered, and dancers mature into old scarecrows. Dancing, unlike what "Quattrocentro finger" fashions, is done in time. But in this place, contraries (e.g., body and soul, time and eternity) come together temporarily in a harmonious dance quite unlike the frenzied, decentered one which concluded the poem. Here nature, symbolized by the body, is not denied or sacrificed to the spirit, symbolized by nuns worshipping images (lines 49–50). In this place, wisdom becomes attainable in a measure different from that of the school children in stanza 1 or the philosophers evoked in stanza 6. Greater than intellect is the wisdom of "simplification" expressed by the dancer.

In "Byzantium," "simplification through intensity" is translated into a ritual fire dance (*CP* 248–49). The poem begins with a gong (echoing the one that accompanied Loïe Fuller's dance in "Nineteen Hundred and Nineteen") striking midnight from the cold, majestic dome of St. Sophia. Immediately, the scene is evacuated of all "unpurged images of day" and "night resonance," compressed into the images of "drunken soldiery" and "night-walkers' song," respectively. These sights and sounds include "All that man is / All mere complexities" (lines 6–7). After the "unpurged images" full of the "fury and mire of human veins" are gone (line 8), an image "bound in mummy-cloth" (line 11) summons "unpurged spirits" to engage in an eschatological dance in stanza 4 which will liberate them from the wheel of endless reincarnations and refine them into ultimate essence.

> At midnight on the Emperor's pavement flit
> Flames that no faggot feeds, nor steel has lit,
> Nor storm disturbs, flames begotten of flame,
> Where blood-begotten spirits come
> And all complexities of fury leave,
> Dying into a dance,
> An agony of trance,
> An agony of flame that cannot singe a sleeve.
>
> (lines 25–32)

Kermode thinks the stylized fire image was inspired by Loïe Fuller's *Danse de feu*. Fuller reportedly shook and twisted "in a torrent of incandescent lava, her long dress spouting flame and rolling around in burning spirals" ("Poet and Dancer" 152). One contemporary French writer called her "a nightmare sculpted in red clay. The fire caresses her dress, seizes her entirely, and, inexorable lover, is sated by nothing short of nothingness" (152). But what must have sparked Yeats's imagination about the dance was the image of Fuller standing unconsumed, smiling enigmatically in the flames. Fuller, as she appeared in *Danse de feu,* was another example of the living body/dead face—a figure to Yeats, like the "superhuman" in the poem and Byzantine art in general, of a synthesis between art and nature.

Readings of "Byzantium," though various, usually fall into one of two camps: the poem is either about the creative process itself, or is an attempt to verbalize a mystical experience. In both interpretations, the dance is primary. Along with the dome in stanza one and the golden bird in stanza 3, it symbolizes or stands

Loïe Fuller's *Danse de feu,* a synthesis between art and nature; "An agony of flame that cannot singe a sleeve." *Courtesy of the Dance Collection, New York Public Library for Performing Arts, Astor, Lenox, and Tilden Foundations.*

for the ordering principle in art, as opposed to the fury, mire, and complexities of nature. This ordering principle is always changing; for all art (like dance) is never really a finished product or artifact but always an ongoing process in which the artist is inextricably linked to his creation. Yeats, remember, assumes we cannot differentiate the dancer from the dance. According to Edward Engleberg, all the images in the poem are developed in terms of flux and stasis (148). The "blood-begotten" spirits, for example, are purged by "Dying into a dance" (line 30), or movement, which is also an "agony of trance" (line 31), or stillness. The flood or tide of the last stanza is broken by the order of the smithies, but what they create—the marbles of the dancing floor—change their pattern as the sea waves break over them ("Those images that yet / Fresh images beget" lines 38–39). And finally in stanza 5, the arrivals once more of the newly dead riding on the backs of warm-

blooded dolphins "break" the quiet of the city with their exuberant arches and loops through a generative, "dolphin-torn, . . .
gong-tormented sea" (line 40).

Dancing in the poem serves a ritualistic function as well. The
intensity of the experience is emphasized by the repetition of the
word "agony" and the alliterative link between "dying" and
"dance." The heavily-stressed rhyme-words at the line-breaks
mimic the sound of stamping feet: "Dying into a dance, / An
agony of trance." Whether this ghostly dance is painful or pleasurable for its participants is left characteristically equivocal.
"Agony" usually denotes pain. But it could be used in the sense
of an "agony of ecstasy" or a transcendent moment of mystical
radiance, thus connoting pleasure. In using such apparent con-
tradictions like the cold-fire oxymoron mentioned earlier, Yeats is
trying to unify all antinomies (life/death, pain/pleasure) and
express in language an experience which fundamentally eludes it.[13]

The real dance in "Byzantium" occurs in the play of its language. Like those "unpurged spirits" riding dolphin-back between
water and air, Donald Ross notes how the reader is suspended
among the endless qualifications of anaphoric images or the rhetorical device of repeating words in successive clauses (293–305):

> Before me floats an image, man or shade,
> Shade more than man, more image than a shade;
>
> . . . .
>
> Miracle, bird or golden handiwork,
> More miracle than bird or handiwork,
>
> (lines 9–10, 17–18)

Ross also points out how the same images are subject to subtly
shifting syntactic emphases as either clauses or appositives and participles: "*complexities* of mire and blood" (line 24), "*complexities*
of fury" (line 29), "furies of *complexity*" (line 37), "complexities of
mire" (line 24) versus "mere *complexities*" (line 7), "*fury* and the
mire" (line 8), "*mire* of human veins" (line 8). He concludes that
verbal echoes, rather than semantic meaning, link images together

in the poem and account for their rich associations. Just as Fuller created the illusion that her evolving shapes had a will of their own, the images in "Byzantium" *appear* to have no external agent acting upon them. Instead, they are self-generating: flames beget flames and images beget images. Even the cluster of transitive verbs in stanza 4 are presented negatively: "no faggot feeds, nor steel has lit" (line 26), "no storm disturbs" (line 27), no flame "can singe a sleeve" (line 32).

Like Fuller's unnatural, stylized fire, none of these images signify anything "out of nature." "Byzantium," of all the dance poems, illustrates best the prose passage in *Autobiographies,* in which Yeats makes the rather startling aesthetic identification with Mallarmé's Salomé rather than with her sacrificial prophet/victim. The strange, self-reflexive imagery in "Byzantium" is like an "idol-atrous mirror" of the imaginary images dancing in the poet's mind. Like "some Hérodiade . . . dancing seemingly alone," these images are (in the poet's words) "separate from everything heterogeneous and casual, from all character and circumstance" (321).

The Poet Grown Old
Just Looks at the Dancers:
1930–38

Dancing in Yeats's final poems no longer resonates with quite the apocalyptic fury it did earlier, nor does the dancer continue to cast quite as powerful a spell over the poet. The speaker in "Those Dancing Days Are Gone" is gay in spite of resembling a mutilated scarecrow too old and stiff to dance (*CP* 266). An older Crazy Jane (in "Crazy Jane Grown Old Looks at the Dancers"), while envious of a younger couple's passionate dancing, is more resigned to her role as spectator than the insecure narrator of "Among School Children." There is, in short, no overwhelming desire of an isolated "I" to join in the dance of a collective "We." The dancing space has also contracted. Instead of the cosmic settings of "Nineteen Hundred and Nineteen" and "Byzantium," the dance returns to a private performance on a seashore by a young, mortal female. But her dancing is not the pure expression of independence and innocence that it was formerly. In "Sweet Dancer" (1937) and "A Crazed Girl" (1936), it signifies a state bordering on madness (*CP* 296, 303).

Both of the poems are about Margot Ruddock, who was not a dancer but an actress Yeats had met in 1934 when he was sixty-nine and she twenty-seven. Just before meeting her, Yeats had submitted to the Steinach operation for sexual rejuvenation. The operation gave him a burst of energy, which he lavished on Margot; he encouraged her to write poetry, introduced her to writers and theater people, sent her to the British choreographer Frederick Ashton for dancing lessons, and through his friend, Shree Purohit Swami, converted her to mysticism. They also corresponded frequently (Jeffares, *A New Biography* 324). A few years after they met, Ruddock suffered a nervous breakdown and tried to drown herself. Yeats related the incident in a letter to Olivia Shakespear dated May 1936:

> A girl who is quite a beautiful person . . . walked in at 6:30 . . . and said she had come to find out if her verse was any good. I had known her for some years and told her to stop writing as her technique was getting worse. She went out in pouring rain . . . and thought that if she killed herself her verse would live instead of her. Went to the shore to jump in and then thought that she loved life and began to dance.
> (quoted, Jeffares, *A New Biography* 366)

In both poems Ruddock is memorialized into the ranks of the Beautiful Dancer archetype, along with the numerous other girls "[the poet's] unremembering nights" held "fast." She is also a tragic figure, like Hamlet, Lear, Cordelia, and other dramatic personae who preoccupied Yeats in this last phase. The subject of "Sweet Dancer," the speaker admits, dances to escape from either "bitter youth," "her crowd," or "her black cloud" (lines 4, 5, 6).

But we are not to justify her being taken away by "strange men" and say "she is happy being crazy" (line 17). Rather, she is happy because she is dancing. What appears to be madness, according to Hazard Adams, is really some supersensual illumination, some incommunicable sense of wonder or glow on her face that is all sweetness and light. The charge of madness is "an affront to the poet's symbolism, which has frequently identified the dance with the perfect antithetical condition. The happiness is the dance itself; just as gaiety is the mask" (224).

It is fitting that the last dancer to appear in Yeats's poetry is none other than Helen of Troy in "Long-Legged Fly" (*CP* 339). Although she had frequently been one of Yeats's subjects, like the other two emblematic figures—Caesar and Michelangelo—who flank her in the first and third stanzas of the poem, this is the first time the *femme fatale* dances: "her feet practice a tinker shuffle / Picked up on the street" (lines 17–18).[14] In the eight lines she is allotted, Helen sums up most of the traits of the Yeatsian dancer. Her likeness to Salomé, for example, is unmistakable. Both stand for the antithetical, subjective fifteenth phase in Yeats's system. Both fulfill their roles as the unthinking and unknowing destroyers of the coldly intellectual civilization that Caesar represents. Helen "thinks . . . / That nobody looks" and performs her dance in a "lonely place" in a kind of creative trance purely for her own emotional and physical pleasure (lines 15–16, 14). Like all of Yeats's dancers, she is "part woman, three parts child" in her innocence and passivity (line 15). Helen does not act like Caesar or create like Michelangelo, but fulfills her destiny just by being who she is. The same simile embedded in a ballad refrain caps her stanza, as it does the others: "Like a long-legged fly upon the stream / Her mind moves upon silence" (lines 19–20). If by "stream" Yeats means the traditional metaphor for time, Helen's dance—like Niamh's, the faeries', and all the dancers' in between—is a symbol of immortality. For just as the water strider, or long-legged fly, gives the appearance of walking, standing, or hovering *over* rather than being immersed *in* the "stream of time," Helen suspends time in her silent absorption of the dance.

Conclusion

From Helen of Troy to a faery band, the dancer sparked Yeats's imagination for over forty years. Just to enumerate her various permutations is to get some idea of the symbol's richness and importance, for the dancer meant different things to the poet in different periods. His earliest landscapes are peopled with pagan Celts "married to rock and hill" through their ecstatic "unearthly" dancing. When he turned to writing about real people in his contemporary landscape, the dancer became the generic title he bestowed on several unattainable women, from Iseult Gonne to Margot Ruddock. During the period of *A Vision,* she became a cosmic dancer, symbolizing absolute beauty and unity of being. She taught him about the value of trance as a vehicle for touching the spiritual world. And from her blank, enigmatic expression, she taught him about impersonality in art.

Sometimes she meant different things in poems written from the same period. Her presence could be fiendish and sinister in one poem, like "Nineteen Hundred and Nineteen," and beneficial and angelic in the next, like "Among School Children." Or she could be morally indifferent, like the dancer in "The Double Vision of Michael Robartes" and the Salomé described in *A Vision,* "receiving the Prophet's head in her indifferent hands." In shaping his image, Yeats sought his inspiration behind the footlights of the European stage and found such luminaries as Michio Ito, Ninette de Valois, Ruth St. Denis, and Loïe Fuller. But he also reached beyond the footlights and fused his Western dancer with Eastern aesthetics and mysticism. Like the Hindu god Shiva, Yeats's dancer is both a creative and destructive force. In her Eastern cast, she symbolized the Oneness underlying spirit and matter and the unity of permanence behind the world of appearances and flux.

T. S. Eliot: "A Dancer Before God"

"I would believe only in a god who could dance."

Nietzsche,
Thus Spoke Zarathustra

For all his reserve, T. S. Eliot was a connoisseur of dance. Admittedly, there are no beautiful dancers adorning Eliot's poetry as figures of a nondiscursive unified sensibility as there are in Yeats. Moths dance ("The Burnt Dancer"), bears dance ("Portrait of a Lady"), and cats dance *(Old Possum's Book of Practical Cats)*, but when a woman dances ("Whispers of Immortality") she is disparagingly likened to a "Brazilian jaguar" with a "rank feline smell." Yet Eliot loved the new dance the Russian ballet brought to Europe and was influenced by two of its leading male stars, Vaslav Nijinsky and Léonide Massine, whom he saw respectively in Paris from 1910 to 1911 and London from 1919 to 1924. Nijinsky was a subliminal inspiration for much of Eliot's verse, just as Massine was a catalyst behind many of his aesthetic speculations. Their dancing was learned and practiced, never instinctual. It required the memory of reiterated movements and constituted a refinement, control, and transcendence of the body, a triumph over the limitations of the self.

Nijinsky haunts the early unpublished poem "The Death of Saint Narcissus" (1915) in which a martyr-figure performs a *danse macabre* in the desert while burning arrows pierce his flesh. And while Eliot missed Nijinsky's choreographic score for *Le Sacre du printemps* in Paris, there is an uncanny resemblance between the ballet's atavistic, dehumanized masses and *The Waste Land*'s hordes of automatons wandering aimlessly through debased rituals. In addition, central images in "The Hollow Men," "Burnt Norton," and "Little Gidding" derive from ballets that have become virtually synonymous with the great dancer, like *Petrouchka, Narcisse,* and *Le Spectre de la rose.*

In numerous reviews and essays for *The Dial* and *The Criterion,* Eliot singled out Massine for exemplifying the virtues of the new ballet. The primary one was the impersonality Massine exuded in performance. Through him, Eliot came to see how the dancer's impersonality was the result of a self-discipline and self-sacrifice to a four-hundred-year-old tradition in which past and present exist simultaneously. Eliot also perceived how the rhythmic and ritual element in ballet worked on the unconscious and tapped the spiritual for art. As a result, ballet became his ideal model for a new poetic drama.

Eliot's published correspondence reveals that he loved to dance himself. Reportedly, he once blurted at a dinner party that only two things really mattered in life: brandy and dance (Bergonzi 34). Frequenting ballet concerts and dance halls, in fact, highlight Eliot's youthful social life. Affected by the excitement engendered by the Ballets Russes in Paris on many intellectuals he befriended there, like Alain-Fournier and Jacques Rivière, Eliot signed up for dancing lessons after his return to Harvard in 1911 (Gordon, *Early Years* 54). Writing his cousin Eleanor Hinkley in 1915 from Oxford, he confessed that he attended dance halls regularly for the relief that dancing provided from the intellectual rigors of graduate studies. After settling in London in 1919, Eliot invited Mary Hutchinson, a member of the Bloomsbury crowd, to come dancing "at a place near Baker Street. They teach the new dances and steps, which I don't know and want to learn" (*Letters* 275).[1]

At one of these dance halls, Eliot met his future wife, Vivienne Haigh-Wood, who had some training in ballet. He admitted to his cousin that he was attracted to Vivienne because she was liberated, meaning she smoked and "was a very good dancer" (97). Brigit Patmore, another Bloomsbury member, recalled an incident between the two in the early years of their marriage that suggests Eliot took Vivienne's dancing seriously. They were in a drugstore when Vivienne suddenly decided to ape the Russian ballerina Tamara Karsavina. She rose on one leg, extended the other in arabesque, and held out her arm for her husband to support her. Eliot, eschewing his typical embarrassment, "watched Vivienne's feet with ardent interest whilst he supported her with real tenderness" (Patmore 85–86).

Both the attraction and the tenderness, unfortunately, were short-lived. Because he identified Vivienne as a dancer, his subsequent marital disillusionment and his alleged sexual problems may have spawned the derogatory portrayal of female dancers who make brief appearances in the early poetry. As these poems make clear, Eliot harbored an extreme distaste for the sexual connotations of dance. His female dancers are mistresses of deceit and artifice; their dancing is pointless and sterile. They easily fit into Lyndall Gordon's classification of Eliot's early poetic treatment of women in general as either "Laforguian butts of ironic dismissal" or "butts of a sense of sin" (Bush 14).

Included in Gordon's first category is the oblique, ironic allusion to Salomé's dancing before Herod in "The Love Song of J. Alfred Prufrock" (*SP* 14). Vivienne was not responsible, for Eliot wrote the poem between 1909 and 1911 a few years before the couple met, though he probably came across the biblical dancer several times from his exposure to Yeats, Symons, Mallarmé, and Laforgue. The image of decapitation ("Though I have seen my head [grown slightly bald] / brought in upon a platter") is a parodic objective correlative of Prufrock's fractured psyche. The power of Salomé's dancing over him is, he confesses, "no great matter." It will neither lead to a new religious dispensation ("I am no prophet") nor resonate with a wealth of artistic associations, as it did for Yeats. Like the other females in the poem, Salomé poses a threat to his vanity. In unmasking the "bald spot in the middle of [his] hair," or the tell tale signs of mortality, Salomé reduces death to mere social embarrassment.

Nancy Ellicott's social dancing in "Cousin Nancy" (1915) is an object of derision rather than fear to the impersonal voice that narrates the poem. Written at Oxford, the poem was one of a series of satirical vignettes on contemporary mores and New England manners, presumably between relatives and people the poet knew in Boston and Cambridge. Cousin Nancy's flaunting of her ability to do "all the modern dances," like her cigarette smoking and her "breaking," or domesticating, the New England hills with her horseback riding, superficially suggest a Yankee independence and individuality. However, they prove to be barren acts of rebellion.

> Miss Nancy Ellicott smoked
> And danced all the modern dances;
> And her aunts were not quite sure how they felt about it,
> But they knew that it was modern.
> (*Complete Poems and Plays* 17–18)

In the last stanza, Eliot, borrowing a line from George Meredith's "Lucifer in Starlight," alludes to Matthew Arnold and Ralph Waldo Emerson as a mock-angelic "army of unalterable law." "Matthew and Waldo" keep "watch" on Nancy, not as voyeurs but as metonymies for the dead books adorning the room in which she dances. The frivolity of her dancing is highlighted by their grave, intellectual guardianship of Victorian culture. Their graveness, in turn, is subverted by reducing them to their first and middle names, and their frozen watch over Nancy on "glazen" or tarnished "shelves" proves ineffectual. Short on foresight, they could not "see" the consequences of their liberal sanctioning of self-expression, which resulted in Nancy's liberated dancing, or what Lawrence would label the "bouncingly copulative" social dances of the twenties.

The association between sterile female dancing and modernity continues in Eliot's allusion to Russian ballerina "Grishkin" in the 1918 poem "Whispers of Immortality" (*SP* 42–43). Grishkin's portrayal as a seductive, high-class prostitute is Eliot's harshest indictment of a female dancer. Like Salomé in "Prufrock," Eliot neutralizes her "deadliness" by turning it into a pun the seventeenth century was fond of making between death and the climax of the sexual act. Her portrait in the second half of the poem follows a dramatic rendering of what Eliot referred to in "The Metaphysical Poets" (1921) as the seventeenth century's unified sensibility: Elizabethan and Jacobean poets like Webster and Donne could feel their thoughts or, conversely, think through their senses. Because they could do so, they knew the senses' limitations. Modern men, however, are "out of joint" with themselves as well as with the past. They are thus reduced to the "scampering marmoset," or monkey, which is instinctively drawn to Grishkin's "maisonette" to experience *le petit mort* at the hands of the "couched" and ready to pounce "Brazilian jaguar." Grishkin's trap is based on the deceitful cultivation of cosmetic allure. Her "friendly bust" (compared to Webster's "breastless creatures under ground") is "uncorseted." It holds out the "promise" only of "pneumatic bliss" for the speaker, who is blind to the "pneuma," or soul, in her body. Her "Russian eye / Is underlined for emphasis" to create an illusion of beauty, where the realistic eyes on the corpses in the first half of the poem have decayed into "daffodil bulbs." "Abstract Entities / Circumambulate her charm" in a parody of the notion that metaphysical perceptions originate in physical experience.

The poem is even more interesting for what it reveals about the poet's divided sensibility at the time. Neither his published correspondence nor his biographers reveal the reason for Eliot's deeply felt repulsion toward "Grishkin," who was actually Serafima Astafieva, a Maryinsky-trained graduate of the Ballets Russes who settled in London, opened a leading ballet school in 1914, and was responsible for churning out such English luminaries of the company as Anton Dolin and Alicia Markova. Even Ezra Pound, who brought Astafieva and Eliot together, questioned the latter's harsh treatment of the dancer years later in his *Pisan Cantos*.[2]

On the other hand, the male dancer in "The Death of Saint Narcissus" (an unpublished poem written between 1914 and 1915) is morbidly self-absorbed yet treated sympathetically (*The Waste Land* 92–97).[3] Narcissus is a self-flagellating religious martyr who dances in the desert to transcend his flesh. Like Prufrock, he suffers from solipsism and a fractured psyche. Wherever Narcissus wanders in the natural world only serves to reflect back to him the beauty of his body parts. The wind causes him to feel his limbs: "his legs smoothly passing each other" and "his arms crossed over his breast." Walking in the meadows, he is "stifled and soothed by his own rhythm." The river makes him sensitive to the "pointed corners of his eyes" and the "tips of his fingers." When Narcissus walks in the city, he sees other people reduced to their lower extremities. Like Dante's stumbling on the damned buried in ice in *The Inferno,* he treads on "convulsive thighs and knees." Then he imagines himself in a series of degraded, autoerotic images, where he evolves from a tree ("[t]wisting its branches" and "tangling its roots") to a fish ("[w]rithing in his own clutch") to a "drunken old man" raping himself as a "young girl" (who at the end knows "the taste of her own whiteness" and the "horror of her own smoothness").

As both "old man" and "young girl," simultaneously experiencing the antithetical roles of violator and violated, Narcissus combines the image of Salomé the aggressor with the Baptist, her passive victim. For unlike Prufrock, Narcissus is an aspiring prophet who tries to turn the liability of his narcissism into an asset. We are told he had been "struck down" by the knowledge of his own beauty and "could not live men's ways" and so instead became a "dancer before God." He escapes humanity and secludes himself in the desert, where his dancing gives him a momentary feeling of unity and sensual pleasure. While there, Narcissus dances for the pleasure/pain of God's arrows penetrating his bleeding flesh. However, the poem ends ambiguously with the suggestion that Narcissus may have been self-deluded. He turns "green, dry and stained / With the shadow in his mouth," ultimately becoming a "dancer to [instead of before] God."

Critics have traced Narcissus's roots to several literary and biblical sources.[4] But the most interesting one comes from David Bernstein, who argues that Eliot modeled his character on the tragic life of the Russian ballet dancer Vaslav Nijinsky ("Nijinsky as Source" 71–104). The germ of the poem, according to Bernstein, was planted when Eliot saw Nijinsky in the title role of *Narcisse* during his stay in Paris in 1911. Bernstein links the pointed corners of Narcissus's eyes with Nijinsky's most striking feature: his almond-shaped, Oriental eyes. He draws a parallel between Narcissus's metamorphosis into a young girl raped by an old man and the young Nijinsky's stormy homosexual liaison with the much older impresario Serge Diaghilev. Nijinsky's reputed religious fanaticism and his preoccupation with Tolstoyism (which intensi-fied after he was fired from the company by Diaghilev for eloping with a Hungarian ballerina) are connected to Narcissus's religious yearnings. Nijinsky also referred to himself in his diary as a "dancer to God." Finally, Bernstein links the last two lines of the poem, which refer to Narcissus as a vegetable-like corpse ("green, dry and stained") who "could not live men's ways," with Nijinsky's catatonic withdrawal in his twenties and subsequent institutional-ization in a Swiss sanatorium until his death in 1950. Bernstein conjectures that since Eliot was also confined to a Swiss sanatorium in 1921 while undergoing psychiatric treatment for depression, he could easily have been privy to gossip about the great dancer. Eliot's "tormented view of the post-War world about him might have intensified his curiosity about a man who had . . . succumbed to this vision and retreated into a more beautiful and peaceful world of his own" (101).

When Eliot saw the Ballets Russes again in London in 1919,

Léonide Massine had replaced Nijinsky as Diaghilev's dancer, choreographer, and lover. Eliot's interest in Massine, whom he mentions repeatedly in his critical writings up to the mid-1920s, together with his zealous commitment to the Russian company reinforce Bernstein's speculations.[5] Eliot's correspondence reveals that his hectic juggling of a full-time position at the bank with writing verse and criticism did not hinder him from attending the Ballets Russes, often on successive nights with or without Vivienne; usually he accompanied members of the Bloomsbury group. From January to July 1919, Eliot saw Massine perform his choreography for *The Three-Cornered Hat, La Boutique Fantastique,* and *The Good-Humoured Ladies.* In the summer of 1921, before Eliot left for Lausanne to complete *The Waste Land,* he saw Massine's restaging of Nijinsky's choreography for *Le Sacre du printemps.* In a letter dated April 1922, after seeing the Ballets Russes at the Coliseum, he wrote Mary Hutchinson that he thought Massine "more brilliant and beautiful than ever. . . . I quite fell in love with him. I want to meet him more than ever, and he is a genius" (*Letters* 523). Two months later, after Hutchinson arranged a meeting between the two, Eliot wrote back to her expressing his gratitude and the hope that he would soon see Massine again (529).

Even after Massine broke with Diaghilev to form his own company, Eliot extolled the dancer's virtues. Chief among these is what Eliot saw as Massine's "impersonality," the same quality Mallarmé had isolated in the ballerinas of the Paris Opéra and Loïe Fuller's abstract shapes and Yeats in Japanese dancer Michio Ito's immobile expression. Mallarmé's dancers, we recall, were not women but vessels filled with abstract, preliterate suggestions. In "Tradition and the Individual Talent," Eliot defined the ideal poet as an impersonal vessel of literary tradition, one who has "not a 'personality' to express, but a particular medium." His progress as an artist is "a continual self-sacrifice, a continual extinction of personality" (*Selected Essays* 7–9). Ironically, Eliot found his ideal poet in the dancer Massine, who extinguished his own personality within ballet's international, four-hundred-year-old tradition. In

Ballets Russes
dancer/choreographer
Léonide Massine, the
model for Eliot's view
of impersonality in art.
*Courtesy of the Dance
Collection, New York Public
Library for Performing Arts,
Astor, Lenox, and Tilden
Foundations.*

"Dramatis Personae" (1923), Eliot called him the "greatest actor
in London . . . the most completely unhuman, impersonal and
abstract." Eliot added that "the difference between the conventional gesture of the ordinary stage, which is supposed to *express*
emotion, and the abstract gesture of Massine, which *symbolizes*
emotion," was enormous.[6] In his 1924 essay "Four Elizabethan
Dramatists," Eliot must have been thinking of Massine when he
wrote:

> Any one who has observed one of the great dancers of the
> Russian school will have observed that the man or the
> woman whom we admire is a being who exists only during
> the performances, that it is a personality, a vital flame which
> appears from nowhere, disappears into nothing and is com-
> plete and sufficient in its appearance. It is a conventional
> being, a being which exists only in and for the work of art
> which is the ballet. . . . The differences between a great
> dancer and a merely competent dancer is in the vital flame,
> that impersonal, and, if you like, inhuman force which tran-
> spires between each of the great dancer's movements. (95)

Massine no doubt influenced Eliot's admiration for the discipline of dance, which he equated with religious asceticism in "Narcissus." Like the Catholic Church, the ballet's authoritarian and hierarchical structure and unified point of view directed and sanctioned the individual member's self-sacrifice. In one issue of *The Criterion,* Eliot exhorted the public to continue supporting Diaghilev because it "was necessary that there should be *one* ballet, and *one* school to supply it, and *one* man at the head of it" [emphasis added].[7] In "A Dialogue on Dramatic Poetry" (1928), speaker "B" reiterates that the strength of ballet lies in its tradition and training. It is "an askesis . . . which ascends for several centuries. . . . any efficient dancer has undergone a training which is like a moral training." "E" (Eliot) agrees and adds that the dance is "a system of physical training, of traditional, symbolical and highly skilled movements. It is a liturgy of very wide adaptability" (34–35).

The ballet was important to Eliot for other reasons besides the impersonality and moral training of its dancers. He perceived a spiritual dimension in the art that was similar to Mallarmé's view of the dance as sacred rite: "the mysterious and holy interpretation of our innermost being" (Mallarmé 63). Eliot tried to account for the sense of awe and terror that ballet evoked in an audience, or its defamiliarization of everyday reality into "something rich and strange."[8] Thinking that primitive man also must have experienced some of this mystery when he danced, Eliot studied anthropologists like Jane Harrison who were interested in the relationship between art and rituals and the basic impulses in man that gave rise to both. As a result, Eliot was convinced that primitive dance or ritual was not only the source of ballet: it was the origin of all art and religion.

Eliot's basically anthropological view of dance became integral to other ideas he had been formulating about the mystical similarities between immediate experience and primitive experience, the continuity of past and present, and the nature of the unconscious. From Bradley, for example, Eliot derived the notion that our world comes to us as a finite center of immediate experience, which we subsequently separate and fragment into objects, selves, emotions, and thoughts. He interpreted Bradley's notion of immediate experience as an intense feeling of unity, a still point arrested out of time that was similar to Yeats's notion of unity of being or Virginia Woolf's "exquisite moments of being." For Eliot, such "moments" or "unities" were mystical in nature and gave fleeting intimations of the Absolute, which Eliot interpreted in Bradley's system as "God." According to William Skaff, Eliot was thus able to identify immediate experience with a primitive consciousness, which lives on in modern man as part of his unconscious (66–67).

From his readings in psychology, Eliot derived a theory of the unconscious that he connected to dance. Basically, he thought the unconscious consisted of three interrelated and overlapping categories or dimensions: physiological, psychological, and metaphysical. The physiological unconscious was that area where bodily functions like the circulatory and neurological systems operated without our being aware of them. One dances, for example, because of an innate sense of rhythm located in the nervous system. The neurological system, however, is that part of our physiology directly related to brain activity and therefore related to thoughts and emotions. Thus the physiological dimension was continuous with the psychological unconscious. Eliot was no Freudian. The unconscious did not consist of the Id or repressed sexual deviant impulses as in psychoanalytic theory. His unconscious was a variation of Jung's theory of the collective unconscious, a repository of universal myths and symbols. Eliot added that this unconscious was not only collective, but historical; the deeper one dug, the more primitive the experience latent there. At the deepest level, one would recover the undifferentiated wholeness and unity of immediate experience, which Eliot characterized as the metaphysical unconscious.

James Frazer's *The Golden Bough* also convinced Eliot that the past was continuous with the present in the unconscious. Eliot described Frazer's work as both "a collection of entertaining myths and . . . a revelation of that vanished mind of which our mind is a continuation."[9] Frazer's hero-gods underwent violent deaths and resurrections at sacred places from which they continued to exercise their powers at festivals that annually re-enacted their drama. In this way, Osiris, Attis, and Adonis, who were originally vegetation gods, ensured an order or continuity in nature as well as in society. Eliot understood the rituals associated with them to be similar to the ritual eating of Christ during the Eucharist. He postulated that the death/rebirth myth was innate and formed part of the structure of the psychological unconscious, just as dance was innate in the physiological part.

Eliot synthesized the relationship between dance rhythms and religious impulses in an article entitled "The Ballet," written for *The Criterion*. "Anyone who wishes to understand the 'spirit' of dancing must start by examining dance in 'primitive' tribes or amongst developed peoples like the Tibetans and the Javanese," he wrote. One must also consider:

> the evolution of Christian and other liturgy. (For is not the High Mass—as performed, for instance, at the Madeleine in Paris—one of the highest developments of dancing?) And finally, he should be able to track down the secrets of rhythm in the (still undeveloped) science of neurology.[10]

What the critic should not do is give logical reasons for the origin of dance. In another essay, Eliot criticized Dr. W. O. E. Oesterley's study of primitive religious dances because its author fell into "the common trap of interpretation, by formulating intelligible reasons for the primitive dancer's dancing." Oesterley claimed that "the origin of the sacred dance was the desire of early man to imitate what he conceived to be the characteristics of supernatural powers."

> It is equally possible to assert that primitive man acted in a certain way and then found a reason for it. An unoccupied person, finding a drum, may be seized with a desire to beat

it; but unless he is an imbecile he will be unable to continue beating it, and thereby satisfying a need (rather than a "desire"), without finding a reason for so doing.[11]

Eliot implies that the origin of ritual dance cannot be interpreted as a logical or practical need, since the origin is prior to interpretation or reason. Primitive man beat his drum because of a prelogical desire to do so.

Primitive peoples responded to the rhythm in their bodies by participating in a collective mystical experience. Eliot thought that since artists were somehow closer to the primitive than their contemporaries, they could reintegrate dance rhythms and rituals into another art form and stimulate once again the dormant religious impulses residing in modern peoples' unconscious.[12] Poets could achieve this because of their "auditory imagination," which Eliot defined in a later essay as the primitive, prelogical instinct for "syllable and rhythm, penetrating far below the conscious levels of thought and feeling" (*Use of Poetry and Criticism* 111).

During the period Eliot was formulating his ballet-inspired theories on rhythm and ritual in the late 1910s and early 1920s, he began to work them out poetically in *The Waste Land* in 1921 and again in "The Hollow Men" in 1925. Dance is not the pure image that will surface after Eliot's religious conversion of 1927 in *Four Quartets*. Rather, both poems contain many instances of antidance imagery or *danse macabre*, like the "crowds of people, walking round in a ring," the "living dead flow[ing] over London Bridge," the "hooded hordes, swarming / Over endless plains" in *The Waste Land* (*SP* 52, 53, 65) and the vacant gestures and aimless circling around the "prickly pear" in "The Hollow Men" (*SP* 79).

Both poems, however, are kindred spirits to two famous Ballets Russes productions. Nijinsky's choreographic experimentation for *Le Sacre du printemps*, as mentioned previously, vanished with his dismissal from the company, and Eliot frankly admitted that he was disappointed in Massine's romantic restaging.[13] But in Stravinsky's music, especially its dissonance and abrupt juxtapositions of modern and folk material, Eliot found a paradigm for the way the complexities and banalities of contemporary life could be rendered into "something rich and strange." Just as Stravinsky presented a true interpenetration of the present and the past in his metamorphosis of "the rhythm of the Steppes into the scream of the motor horn, the rattle of machinery, the grind of wheels, the beating of iron and steel, the roar of the underground railway, and the other barbaric cries of modern life," *The Waste Land* imposes the fertility myth on the "unreal" city of London and extends it spatially in time back to the linguistic beginnings of western civilization.[14]

Another Stravinsky ballet, *Petrouchka,* informs "The Hollow Men." Valerie Eliot claims that the "hollow" or "stuffed men" were inspired by the marionettes in the ballet, which Eliot saw in Paris with Nijinsky in the title role (Southam 155). Nijinsky/Petrouchka's "human" soul imprisoned in a sawdust body and his impossible love for the Ballerina are correlatives of the hollow men's impotent desire and psychological disintegration. The inhabitants of this dead land, for all their emptiness, are still "Trembling with tenderness" with "lips that would kiss" (*SP* 79). Remembering Eliot's dictum that the artist should "take a form of entertainment and subject it to the process which would leave it a form of art," it is entirely plausible that Eliot was thinking of Petrouchka's disjointed, mechanical gestures when he described the condition of the hollow men as "paralysed force, gesture without motion" (*SP* 77).[15] In both poem and ballet, the failure of the self to achieve an existential freedom results in futility and despair.

The specters of both Nijinsky and Massine return in the *Four Quartets,* where the dance image flits in and out of three of the four poems to convey an elusive, ineffable experience that words alone are incapable of expressing. Dance conveys both "the way up" (eternity) and "the way down" (time) and is related to the particular element associated with each section. In "Burnt Norton" (1936), for instance, the dance is an airy flight of molecules "figured in the drift of the stars" (*Four Quartets* 54). In "East Coker" (1940), it descends to the earth and goes the way of all mutable,

The inspiration behind Eliot's "The Hollow Men" was Nijinsky's marionette in the title role of Fokine's *Petrouchka* for the Ballets Russes (around 1910–11). *Courtesy of the Dance Collection, New York Public Library for Performing Arts, Astor, Lenox, and Tilden Foundations.*

material things into "flesh, fur and faeces." In "Little Gidding" (1943), the dance is apotheosized and fused to the purgative, "refining" fire that destroys in order to create. Instead of a phoenix rising from the ashes, Eliot conjures up *Le Spectre de la rose*, a ballet made famous by Nijinsky's spectacular leap from the stage up through a bedroom window.

In "Burnt Norton," the dance is first evoked in the fifteen-line symbolist lyric which begins the second movement.

> Garlic and sapphires in the mud
> Clot the bedded axle-tree.
> The trilling wire in the blood
> Sings below inveterate scars
> Appeasing long forgotten wars.
> The dance along the artery
> The circulation of the lymph
> Are figured in the drift of stars
> Ascend to summer in the tree

> We move above the moving tree
> In light upon the figured leaf
> And hear upon the sodden floor
> Below, the boarhound and the boar
> Pursue their pattern as before
> But reconciled among the stars.
>
> (lines 47–61)

These lines echo the elaborate cosmic dance which underlines Sir John Davies's Elizabethan poem "Orchestra," or "A Poem of Dancing" (1596).[16] Davies's use of the dance conceit enabled him to seamlessly weave in and out of abstract concepts and concrete images. In "Orchestra," dance is the natural and proper activity of every level of being moving harmoniously in a universal hierarchy. The universe is depicted as a great dancing wheel, with love or stillness at its unmoving center or hub. As the stars and spheres revolve in a perpetual dance around heaven's "axle-tree," love dances in every human pulse and vein ("Orchestra" stanzas 36, 64, 106).

The "garlic and sapphires" passage in "Burnt Norton" also depicts a rhythmic design throughout the universe with close correspondences between different levels of being: mineral, vegetable, animal, human, and planetary. The continuity and recurrence of life on earth, figured in "the dance along the artery" and "the circulation of the lymph," is paralleled in the images of summer and the cycling of seasons and of space and the cycling of constellations, or "drift of the stars." The "inveterate scars" of human wars parallel the perpetual pursuit of the "boarhound and the boar" on the "sodden floor / Below." The first line's star-shaped "sapphire" mired in the mud is ultimately "reconciled among the stars."

Yet just as the center could not hold in Yeats's universe, stars "drift" in Eliot's world, too, signaling an instability in this passage that contrasts with the unified worldview evoked in Davies's poem. After the first two sentences, grammatical units and images tend to blur. While resembling Ursa Major, or the Great Bear, the "boarhound and boar" do not refer to any known constellation. The "scars" of "forgotten wars" dancing in human arteries receives a heavier emphasis than love pulsing in human veins. Eliot's heavenly axle-tree is earthbound and "clotted" by an incongruous pairing of "garlic and sapphires," all images derived from Mallarmé to evoke the thick palpability of the physical world. For all its seductiveness, this world exists in time and is subject to the laws of mutability.

The wedge-shaped "garlic" and clotted "axle-tree," however, when joined with "moving tree," presage the next stanza's vision of eternity as a still point at the center of a modern wheeling universe.

> At the still point of the turning world. Neither flesh nor
>   fleshless;
> Neither from nor towards; at the still point, there the
>   dance is,
> But neither arrest nor movement. And do not call it fixity,
> Where past and future are gathered. Neither movement
>   from nor towards,
> Neither ascent nor decline. Except for the point, the still
>   point,
> There would be no dance, and there is only the dance.
>
>   (lines 62–71)

Certainly, the serious tone here moves beyond Davies's "light muse" into the realm of metaphysical speculation and mystical experience. Numerous critics have read the passage as a meditation on time and timelessness.[17] Specifically, Eliot's dance at the "still point" is a figure for Bradley's concept of "immediate experience": an increase in consciousness with a concomitant feeling that time has been momentarily suspended. It also has sources in Yeats's Great Wheel, the image of unified reality pictured as two interpenetrating, gyrating cones in *A Vision*. Eliot substitutes the abstract image of the still point for Yeats's dancer, who, in representing the fifteenth stage in his system, signified an escape from time or the cycle of endless reincarnations.

Like a mystical experience, dance cannot be pinned down

by a normal vocabulary or ordinary experience. (One cannot, after all, read a dance in quite the same way as a literary text.) So Eliot, following his dance model, orchestrates a variety of rhetorical devices, like repetitions and paradoxes, with the result that words dance, vibrate, or "trill" around a nondimensional, nontemporal "still point." As in Yeats's "Byzantium," the dance energizes and releases the imaginative potential of words and liberates them from their literal meaning.

In the fifth section of "Burnt Norton," the distinction between eternity and time shifts into a discussion between the eternal Christian Word and the trials and tribulations of the poet who must traffic in ephemeral, time-laden words. Like music, words are only air molecules dancing in time and measure. "Only by the form, the pattern, / Can words or music" (lines 140–41) attain the ideal of a "music heard so deeply / That it is not heard at all" ("The Dry Salvages," 5: 210–11). Like Christ in the desert, the poet is distracted from seeing this pattern by earthly temptations, imaged in the "crying shadow in the funeral dance" (line 157). The funeral dance, the antithesis of the still point, anticipates the impersonal funeral dance of time in "East Coker," which belongs to no one, "for there is no one to bury" (line 112). The funeral dance, or *danse macabre,* also recalls the earlier debased rituals or antidances in *The Waste Land* and "Hollow Men," which were played out on a worldly desert of spiritual values. It resonates also with the deathly desert dance before God of Narcissus, who "could not live men's ways" and willfully exchanged the torments of an illusive temporal world—the "disconsolate chimera"—for a more beautiful, private vision of eternity.

Following closely upon the heels of the funeral dance is the marriage dance in "East Coker," section 1, which signifies fertility, rebirth—"the coupling of man and woman" in harmonious "concorde" with the natural world (line 44). Earlier, Eliot nodded to an Elizabethan authority on dance; here he quotes directly from a Tudor one: his ancestor, Sir Thomas Elyot. Elyot's treatise *The Boke Named the Governour* (1531) equated various types of dancing with moral and social virtues.[18] In "East Coker," "daun-singe, signifying matrimonie" is:

> A dignified and commodiois sacrament.
> Two and two, necessarye coniunction,
> Holding eche other by the hand or the arm
> Whiche betokeneth concorde. Round and round the fire
> Leaping through the flames, or joined in circles,
> Rustically solemn or in rustic laughter
> Lifting heavy feet in clumsy shoes,
> Earth feet, loam feet, lifted in country mirth
> Mirth of those long since under earth
> Nourishing the corn. Keeping time,
> Keeping the rhythm in their dancing
> As in their living in the living seasons
> The time of the seasons and the constellations
> The time of milking and the time of harvest
> The time of the coupling of man and woman
> And that of beasts.
>
> (lines 24–45)

Keeping time orders the universe, so that both humans and beasts are in step or "reconciled among the stars." Unlike the meaningless circling of the waste landers and hollow men, the peasants' going "round and round" has purpose: "necessarye coniunction." Eliot's choreographing of this pagan dance to the incantatory rhythms of "Ecclesiastes" illustrates his long-held view of the "primitive" element at the heart of all liturgy.

Yet if we want to see the ancient couples dancing to the "weak pipe and drum," the speaker warns us twice "not to come too close" (line 22). There is an element of unreality in the image of these ghostly, early-sixteenth-century figures dancing in concentric circles around a bonfire ("heart of light") in an open field on a midsummer's eve. Their ritual does not signify a joyous occasion, since the peasants' "rustic laughter" is equated with the "mirth of those long since under the earth" (line 38). Those who

keep time to the rhythm of their bodies, Eliot implies, keep time
to the rhythm of a wheeling, transient universe.

> Feet rising and falling.
> Eating and drinking. Dung and death.
>
> (lines 45–46)

The speaker's abrupt swing in tone from one of enchantment to
somberness indicates that for him the natural or sexual order is a
fragile one. Instead of rebirth and fertility, the mutability scale tips
in favor of death and decay: "Dung and dust." The marriage dance
ultimately goes the way of the funeral one. "The dancers are all
gone under the hill" (line 100).

Eliot's evoking the sexual connotations of dance only to
"bury" them a few lines later suggests he never buried completely
his prudish attitude toward the body—especially when half of those
dancing "bodies" belong to women. Lyndall Gordon likened
Eliot's grave summation of the marriage rite as "dung and dust"
to the "stern voice of denial" of "the Puritan killjoy in Hawthorne's
tale, who rebukes and breaks up the nuptial frolics in 'The Maypole
of Merry Mount'" (*New Life* 98). While Gordon's judgment is
harsh, Eliot's language in this section betrays a certain ambivalence
about even benign fertility rites. The speaker quotes Elyot, who
wrote for a class of aristocrats on the moral virtues culled from
dancing. But he presents us with a picture of peasants, heavy in
"clumsy shoes," engaged in a lot of brusque fumbling with their
mates. Hardly a "dignified" sacrament, their dancing is less graceful than the midnight dance of the "Jellicle Cats" in *Old Possum's
Book of Cats.*

By fusing dance with the purgatorial image of fire, Eliot
attempts in "Little Gidding" (1943), his last quartet, to reconcile
"East Coker"'s earthy, timebound dance with "Burnt Norton"'s
airy eternal one. While treading "the pavement in a dead patrol"
at dusk during a London air raid, the speaker in the second movement meets a "compound ghost," who informs him of the bitter
disillusions attendant on old age and the despair awaiting in hell
for the unrepentant.

> "From wrong to wrong the exasperated spirit
> Proceeds, unless restored by that refining fire
> Where you must move in measure, like a dancer."
>
> (lines 144–46)

Critics have dismantled this compound ghost into several representative voices of tradition. Yet the refining fire that melts away the dross of imperfections in a dance most recalls the flames of Yeats's "Byzantium," in which "blood-begotten" spirits— "Dying in a dance, / An agony of trance"—purge themselves of all "complexities of mire and blood." For both poets, dance serves to order or reconcile such opposites as pleasure/pain, motion/ stillness, and time/eternity and to express in language a mystical experience which eludes rational discourse. For Eliot, this fiery dance is more moral than aesthetic, since it burns away the imperfections of selfish love ("Attachments to self and to things and to persons" line 152), leaving the soul free to experience the divine love he associates with Christ.

The metaphysical implications of the dancer's refining fire, especially as it builds on the previous image of dance as the still point or intersection of time and timelessness, recall Paul Valéry's equating the dance with a flame in "Dance and the Soul" (1921). The dance is capable of evoking "the moment itself" (like the privileged moment of Eliot's immediate experience), which is neither the past nor the future but the instant, which the dancer like the flame renders visible to the eye. The dance, like the flame, is "the proud, ungraspable form assumed by the noblest destruction. What will never happen again happens magnificently before our eyes! What will never happen again must happen in the most magnificent manner possible!" (320)

In the third section of "Little Gidding," the dancer and the flame are linked in the image of the rose. Woven from the element of purifying fire, the rose is a Dantean symbol suggesting the fusion of opposites in a lovers' knot (Traversi 210). John Haywood, Eliot's friend and editor, suggested to the poet that he change line 184— "To summon the spectre of a Rose"—into "ghost of a rose"

Nijinsky in *Le Spectre de la rose* (1911): "Why should we celebrate / These dead men more than the dying? / It is not to ring the bell backward / Nor is it an incantation / To summon the spectre of the Rose" ("Little Gidding"). *Courtesy of the Dance Collection, New York Public Library for Performing Arts, Astor, Lenox, and Tilden Foundations.*

instead. Eliot refused and wrote back to Haywood that he was specifically thinking of the ballet he saw in Paris (one based on a Gautier poem) in which Nijinsky made his famous leap (Gardner 202).[19] The utter abandonment of Nijinsky's movement demonstrated to the poet the "tension between individual tumult and the discipline of set form" (Gordon, *New Life* 125). When asked how he executed the leap, Nijinsky used to say that once he was up in the air, he forgot to come down. But when he did alight, it was always in one of the five prescribed positions of classical ballet.

The image of dance in "Little Gidding," section 5, is a reworking of the language problem in "Burnt Norton," section 5. Here the poet emerges victorious over the slippery, finite words of the funeral dance through his harmonious reconciliation of opposites within the medium of poetry. The marriage of formal and colloquial, archaic and neologistic ("The common word exact without vulgarity, / The formal word precise but not pedantic"), results in:

"The complete consort dancing together" (lines 221–23). Thus dance is ultimately an emblem of successful poetic composition.

"The complete consort dancing together" is also an apt description of how the image in *Four Quartets* recapitulates and unifies Eliot's entire thoughts and feelings on dance. In "Burnt Norton," section 2, his conjectures about the innate appeal of rhythm to the physiological/psychological unconscious are illustrated in the "trilling," singing blood and the "dance along the artery." In the same section, the mystical experience of the timeless moment, which Eliot had equated with Bradley's "immediate experience," is figured as the dance "at the still point of the turning world." In the fifth section, St. Narcissus's dance of religious purification in the desert is abstracted into the impersonal image of "the crying shadow of the funeral dance." "East Coker," section 1, transforms the empty, vacant rituals of *The Waste Land* and "Hollow Men" into the more purposeful (though still imperfect) marriage rites of sixteenth-century peasants. The impersonality and askesis Eliot saw in Massine and Nijinsky's art, finally, underlines "Burnt Norton"'s cosmic dance as well as "Little Gidding"'s purgatorial one.

D. H. Lawrence: Dancing with the "Greater, Not the Lesser Sex"

"Movement never lies. It is a barometer telling the state of the soul's weather to all who can read it."

Martha Graham

Dance revitalized Lawrence's prose rather than his verse. Beginning with *The White Peacock* (1906–11), all but three of his nine lengthy novels contain dance scenes.[1] These scenes illustrate Lawrence's version of impersonality and enact Yeats's insight about the impossibility of differentiating dancer from dance, as individuals lose their egos to the "greater inhuman will" contained in the dance. Lawrence also inherits from Yeats the compelling image of the woman dancing alone. But her treachery is a function of mind rather than body.

Dance, like sex, is important in Lawrence because its physically expressive, nonverbal gestures constitute "blood consciousness" or "phallic consciousness," two terms he uses interchangeably to mean sympathetic awareness, instinct, and intuition, "all the vast vital flux of knowing that goes on in the dark, antecedent to the mind" (Lawrence, *Studies in American Literature* 90).[2] What one knows through the body "overwhelms, obliterates, and annuls mind-consciousness. Mind-consciousness extinguishes blood-consciousness, and consumes the blood" (91). Lawrence felt the two forms of consciousness are inherently antagonistic in humans and that duality is our cross.

Yet he also felt the "moderns" made the burden unduly heavy by actively favoring their mental life over the instinctual life of the body. Lawrence dramatizes this imbalance in fiction as a breakdown in the relationships between the sexes. Because many of his characters cannot connect to each other through a spontaneous give and take of sympathy, they resort to the only means they have: mechanically exerting their wills over each other. Often the will to control, without the guidance of the instincts, results in a total loss of control. Hermione's rationalizations before she smashes Birkin's skull with her lapis lazuli sculpture is an extreme case in point.

Dance in the major fiction serves a therapeutic function by rectifying psychic imbalances between mind and body (also referred to in his essays as the dichotomy between "being" and "knowing" or the "sympathetic" and "voluntary" impulses in humans). His more unbalanced characters end up confronting their repressed urges, like the will to control, which rise to the surface in the impersonal dance. For them, the dance is likely to be a destructive force: Ursula's figurative annihilation of her lover Skrebensky in *The Rainbow* or her sister Gudrun's diabolical dancing in front of a herd of cattle in *Women in Love*. For Lawrence's more mature characters, those who are willing to let go of their egos, the dance is likely to be creative: Kate Leslie's initiation into phallic consciousness or Connie Chatterley's homage to it with her rain-soaked fertility rites in the sacred wood surrounding Wragby Manor.

Biographical Background

Unlike the other three modernists, Lawrence's nomadic existence, living far away from European centers of culture, precluded much contact with theatrical dancing. There are only two occasions on which Lawrence crossed paths with contemporary dancers, and the second was indirectly. The first was at an Armistice party in 1918, in which members of the Bloomsbury group hobnobbed and foxtrotted with Diaghilev, Massine, and Lydia Lopokova. David Garnett records that Lawrence was still in such a funk over the war that he sat on a sofa by himself and hardly spoke to anyone (Nehls 478–79). Shortly afterwards, Lawrence left England for good, settled briefly in Florence, and struck up what was to become a notorious friendship with Maurice Magnus, an eccentric German-American who lived extravagantly, committed suicide, and left his debts for his friends to settle. Magnus had been Isadora Duncan's manager and became the model for Mr. May, the dubious theatrical manager in Lawrence's novel *The Lost Girl*.[3]

Magnus's connection with both Duncan and Lawrence is not totally coincidental, as more than one critic notes an affinity between these two unlikely contemporaries. Raynor Heppenstall refers to Duncan as "the female counterpart of D. H. Lawrence in literature" (Copeland and Cohen 276). To Sandra Gilbert, Duncan's frequent image of herself as the *Magna Mater* or "potent Griselda" is mirrored in Lawrence's "frequently articulated ideas about the primacy of maternity" (Balbert and Marcus 131). The image of floods flowing in great waves is Lawrence's most prevalent figure for the creative female principle in the universe, just as wave images pervade Duncan's dances and writings. Both artists, moreover, glorify the body and share an anatomical view of human psychology. Standing still for hours with her hands folded beneath her breasts, Duncan discovered that the solar plexus reflects the spirit's vision and is the "central spring of all movement" (Kendall 66). To Lawrence, the solar plexus is the "great, magnetic or dynamic centre of first consciousness," which through the mother's navel enforces in the fetus a sympathetic relation with the cosmos (*Fantasia* 221). Duncan and Lawrence were also propagandists and self-exiles who prophetically denounced their places of birth and sought sustaining images in past cultures: Duncan among the ancient Greeks, Lawrence with the Aztecs and Etruscans.

Even if Lawrence never mentions Duncan, there are enough references to other contemporary choreographers in his fiction to suggest he was well aware of the new art. In *The Lost Girl* (1920), for instance, Mr. May (Magnus) engages a dancer for Houghton's Pleasure Palace who bears a remarkable resemblance to symbolist dancer Loïe Fuller. Miss Poppy Traherne, "a lady in innumerable petticoats . . . could whirl herself into anything you like, from an arum lily in green stockings to a rainbow and a catherine wheel and a cup and saucer" (132). Miss Poppy creates her own sets by manipulating fabric: like Fuller, she "twirled till her skirts lifted as in a breeze, rose up and became a rainbow above her now darkened legs" (136).

However, the first "real life" dancer to make a significant appearance in his fiction is none other than Lawrence's father, Arthur, who became the model of the dark, dancing miner Walter Morel in *Sons and Lovers*. Arthur Lawrence was inarticulate, could hardly write, and never read anything but the newspaper, but by all reports was a lively, accomplished dancer. According to Keith Sagar, Lawrence recalled that his father once ran a dancing class and that the only time he ever heard his mother praise his father was for his dancing (15). Arthur inherited his ability from his father, John Lawrence, who was also known for his graceful step (Meyers 11). There are no dancers, to be sure, on the novelist's maternal side. The daughter of a ruined lace manufacturer and pious Congregationalist, Lydia Beardsall inherited her family's puritanical disdain of this idle pastime.

In all likelihood, Lydia discouraged her frail youngest son from dancing as well. As an adult, Lawrence never mentions in his letters taking dancing lessons or attending dances, as Yeats, Eliot, and Williams do. But we are treated to a vivid portrayal of how Lawrence fancied himself dancing through Rupert Birkin, his alter ego in *Women in Love*. Birkin dances on three separate occasions, always alone and joyously, like a satyr in a rapid, quirky movement "he had all to himself" (85). Ursula is "fascinated by the sight of his loose, vibrating body, perfectly abandoned to its own dropping and swinging," yet felt it was an "obscenity, in a man who talked as a rule so very seriously" (160). The differences between Birkin's uninhibited dancing and that of another biographically related character, Cyril Beardsall, the first-person narrator in Lawrence's first novel, are revealing. In *The White Peacock*, Cyril's dancing typifies his provincial Midlands middle-class aspirations and his Pre-Raphaelite tastes. He performs the socially acceptable forms with a refined, well-bred aplomb, but with none of Birkin's inimitable style or freedom. (Cyril, we will see shortly, is more important as a commentator on the dancing of others.)

Besides the fiction, Lawrence often wrote about dance in his travel sketches. In fact, where Eliot fancied himself a ballet critic, Lawrence became a cultural dance historian, trotting around the globe, observing the communal dances of preindustrial cultures and comparing them favorably with the gyrating, "jazzing," and "bouncingly copulative" popular dances of his own day, like the Charleston and tango. In "The Dance," published in *Twilight in Italy* (1916), two Englishwomen dance with Italian peasants and express "a bipolar unity" between southern Dionysian power and a moribund Northern Europe, "working out its last consequences of Christianity" (Foster 184). In another essay, Lawrence mentions his being overcome by a fleeting "sense of religion" watching the "utter dark absorption" of naked men performing the "so-called devil dances in a far-remote jungle in Ceylon" (*Selected Essays* 183). But it was not until he came to America and saw the dances of Southwest Native Americans that he experienced a permanent sense of religion as an "uncontrollable sensual experience, even more so than love" (*Phx* 144). More will be said later of the three essays published in *Mornings in Mexico* (1927), where Lawrence, drawing on Jane Harrison's *Ancient Art and Ritual*, underlines the differences between European spectacle (which includes drama and dance) and Native American dance rites. Finally, in "Making Love to Music," (1927–29), Lawrence describes an ancient tomb painting in which an Etruscan woman illustrates primitive wholeness as she "dances her very soul into existence" (*Phx* 166).

Warming Up:
The White Peacock, Sons and Lovers, and "The White Stocking"

The three major dance scenes in *The White Peacock* consist of traditional social dances depicted in a naturalistic style, which are not, superficially at least, distinguishable from comparable scenes in the novels of Lawrence's English predecessors like Jane Austin and George Eliot. But they do reveal in embryonic form Lawrence's mature treatment of dance starting with *The Rainbow* (1915). Even at this stage, dance functions as a weapon in the service of sexual domination and class discrimination. It also contributes to a cluster of images associated with the white peacock of the title, which Lawrence took from Aubrey Beardsley's illustrations for Oscar Wilde's *Salomé*. In the play, and especially in the drawings, white peacocks are associated with the decadent *femme fatale* dancer.[4]

The White Peacock focuses on the love triangle between a simple farmer, George Saxton, and the hyper-cultivated Lettie Beardsall, Cyril's sister, who ultimately rejects George and marries the son of a rich industrialist, Leslie Tempest. (Cyril has a relationship with Emily, George's sister, which is also doomed to failure.) Lettie is alternately attracted and repelled by George's bulging biceps, masculine independence, and exuberant polka dancing, and he, in turn, is swept away by her dazzling talk and cultural accomplishments, like her ability to play the piano and dance the minuet. George, with his easy male grace and beauty, is the forerunner of such prototypical Laurentian males as Walter Morel, Oliver Mellors, and Don Ramón Carrasco. His affinity with nature is stressed in the mowing scenes, where Cyril remarks on the gracefulness of George's scything: "he swung with a beautiful rhythm from the waist." Cyril admits "there was something exceedingly attractive about the rhythmic body" (93). Lettie is "lissome" and "by nature graceful," too, but unlike George she is willful and follows the dictates of her mind rather than her instincts and is, therefore, Lawrence's first fatal woman.

The first dance scene, which occurs in the wheat fields under a full August moon, reveals the relationships among the five main characters. The moon, which will form an important symbolic cluster with dance in *The Rainbow,* makes Lettie feel like doing the polka. Leslie, characteristically, hates the polka, so Lettie does a "flying" whirl, "hissing through the dead leaves," first with Cyril, then with George. Cyril thinks the polka is "innate in one's feet" (102). The polka, an appropriate form for a pastoral setting, transcends class barriers and is free of rules and restrictions. Caught up in the dizziness of whirling, its participants surrender their individual egos to escape to an impersonal level of pure sensuality. According to Cyril,

> [Lettie and George] spun around the grass . . . he leaped, sprang with large strides, carrying her with him. It was tremendous, irresistible dancing. Emily and I must join, making an inner ring. Now and again there was a sense of something white flying near, and wild past us. Long after we were tired they danced on. At the end, he looked big, erect, nerved with triumph, and she was exhilarated like a Bacchante. (102)

The next dance, occurring inside the Saxton house, dramatizes the mounting sexual and social pressures on the couple. This time George initiates the dance and proceeds to overwhelm Lettie by whirling her around his living room until she collapses from exhaustion. The rest of the family watches anxiously as George's "eyes glowed like coal" and "he was panting in sobs." Lettie, however, has her comeuppance and discomfits George by forcing him to display his clumsiness in a minuet, a dance he is not familiar with. According to Cyril, she "put him through the steps. . . . It was very ridiculous" (149). As opposed to the closed form of the polka, the minuet (which went through a late-nineteenth-century revival) is an open form traditionally performed among the upper classes (Rust 78–79). With its delicately planned geometry of dance steps, it is also the quintessence of dignity and formality. There is no room for individual variation, embellishment, or creativity. Lettie, showing off her cultural refinement, dominates the rest of the scene and bullies Cyril into taking her through two other intricate, set forms—the valeta and mazurka. Then she condescends to teach Emily how to dance.

In the last dance scene in the novel, George surprises Lettie at her twenty-first birthday party by announcing that he's been to Nottingham to learn such upper-class forms as the mazurka, valeta, and minuet. Lettie is impressed but tells him "it's too late." She confesses she cannot help expecting "things"; she was raised to expect them. Foreshadowing Connie Chatterley and her unhappy marriage, Lettie tragically splits herself off from physical life by marrying nondancer Leslie for the mental and social life he offers. Tormented by his passion for Lettie, George eventually destroys himself with alcohol.

As a dancer, Lettie is also obliquely associated with the novel's references to Beardsley's illustrations of Salomé and her white peacocks. According to Robert Gajdusek, Lawrence alludes to white peacocks thirteen times (193), although the first overt mention of them is not made until late in the novel and then by a minor character, the gamekeeper Annabelle, another prototype of the virile Laurentian male. While Annabelle is seated with Cyril in a church graveyard, a peacock with a voluptuous neck and rich tail "glimmering like a stream of coloured stars" perches on the bowed head of a stone angel. Annabelle cries out: "That's the soul of a woman—or it's the devil" (*The White Peacock* 210). The bird reminds him of his first wife, the Lady Crystabel, who got "souly," meaning she steeped herself in culture and idealisms, refused to have children, and eventually got bored with her "good animal" Annabelle. When the bird defecates on the bowed head, the gamekeeper is certain: "Just look! . . . the dirty devil's run her muck over that angel. A woman to the end, I tell you, all vanity and screech and defilement" (210).

In both the novel and Beardsley's drawings, the white peacock is a symbol for the predatory female. But Cyril, in what will have important ramifications for Lawrence's future novels, reverses Salomé's traditional connotations. After Annabelle compares not only his emasculating first wife but all women to peacocks, Cyril agrees but qualifies his statement by adding that the female of the species, the peahen, is white rather than multicolored. Cyril means that the peahen's whiteness renders her less beautiful than the male and sterile as well. Thus, unlike the Wilde/Beardsley Salomé handed down to Yeats, whose excessive beauty was deadly, Lawrence's female dancers are treacherous when they think and, as Annabelle says, fail to be "good animals."

Once Lettie makes a split between her mind and body by marrying Leslie, she, too, is cloaked in peacock imagery.

> She let her cloak slide over her white shoulder and fall with silk splendour of a peacock's gorgeous blue over the arm of the large settee. There she stood, with her white hand upon the peacock of her cloak. . . . She knew her own splendour, and she drew up her throat laughing and brilliant with triumph. (330)

In the earlier polka scene between Lettie and George, Cyril's observing "something white flying near, and wild" refers to one of the thirteen white peacocks noticed in the text. In the dance scene where Lettie uses her mastery of sophisticated steps to show her superiority to George, Cyril compares her to another *femme fatale*, Carmen, the heroine of Gautier's poem, Mérimée's novella, and Bizet's opera. Lettie dances elegantly, he admits, but with a little of "Carmen's ostentation—her dash and devilry" (150). Another oblique association between Lettie and white peacocks occurs when Cyril introduces George to Beardsley's illustrations. George is convinced that if he can show the pictures to Lettie, she will consent to drop Leslie and marry him instead. George, reacting to the erotic element in art nouveau, makes a subliminal identification between Salomé and Lettie, but is blind to the dazzling whiteness of her peacocks. Because she has been out shopping all day for white things for her wedding to Leslie, the magic moment George desires is never consummated.

The next fatal woman—the possessive, Jocasta-like Gertrude Morel of Lawrence's most autobiographical novel, *Sons and Lovers*—is a puritan who shuns dancing. Possibly in unconscious deference to his mother, who was the model for Mrs. Morel, dance is often alluded to, but mostly absent from the text. While not a major theme, it continues to epitomize the conflict between the sexes and social classes. The association between dance and the vital force in nature, hinted at in the pastoral polka dancing between George and Lettie in *The White Peacock,* is strengthened in Lawrence's third novel. This force is free, individualistic, and indeterminate and runs counter to a deterministic force operating in society, which includes the physically crippling environment of the mines, the emotionally crippling Oedipal relationships between Mrs. Morel and her sons, and Mrs. Morel's spiritually crippling Calvinist background.

Ironically, the sensuous dimension of dance is the cause of bourgeois Mrs. Morel's "slip and fall" into the lower classes because of her marriage to a miner. In "The Early Married Life of the Morels," she notices Morel dancing at a Christmas party and is drawn to the "subtle exultation like glamour in his movement."

> Gertrude herself was rather contemptuous of dancing; she had not the slightest inclination towards that accomplish-ment, and had never learned even a Roger de Coverly. She was puritan, like her father, high-minded and really stern. Therefore the dusky, golden softness of this man's sensuous flame of life, that flowed off his flesh like the flame from a candle, not baffled and gripped into incandescence by thought and spirit as her life was, seemed to her something wonderful, beyond her. (*Sons and Lovers* 10)

Dance also functions in the narrative to signify a reversal in the Morels' relationship. Because she "was too much his opposite," Mrs. Morel becomes thoroughly disillusioned after one year of marriage and now reads Morel's dancing as a lack of moral and intellectual fiber. Because "she was superior" and "could not help it," the neighbor ladies enjoy taunting her about Morel's past prowess as a dancer. They tell her about the dancing classes he ran in the Miners' Arms's club-room for five years and how "it was thronged every Tuesday, and Thursday, an' Sat'day—an' there *was* carryin's-on, accordin' to all accounts." The narrator comments: "This kind of thing was gall and bitterness to Mrs. Morel" (13).

Through a combination of factors—his own weakness, his wife's "casting him off," and the physical conditions at the mines—Morel's "sensuous flame" is extinguished early in the marriage. But it is rekindled in his eldest son, William, who "in spite of his mother," inherits his father's passion for dancing. At the same time, he inherits his mother's middle-class aspirations ("getting on") and is encouraged by her to look down on his father as a brutish failure. Gertrude lavishes William, and her younger son Paul, with the displaced erotic passion withheld from Morel. "She saw him a man, young, full of vigour, making the world glow again for her" (47). "Almost, he was like her knight who wore *her* favour in the battle" (79). William is not resilient enough to withstand (as Paul will) the crippling effects of this Oedipal attachment, and the split he makes between his mind and body eventually kills him.

As in the Morels' early relationship, references to dance punctuate the narrative of William's fate and inevitable decline. Like Paul's death in the story "The Rocking-Horse Winner," William's pneumonia and death is ascribed to some eerie, supernatural cause, as if he were being punished for a transgression against his mother that included dancing and sexual disloyalty. After a succession of "flames" come to the house asking for William, Mrs. Morel tells him to keep away "those brazen baggages you meet at dancing-classes" (53). She leaves the house rather than have to face her son costumed as a Highlander for a "fancy-dress ball," even though the ball is a sign of William's upward social mobility (54). As William grows more successful, earning thirty shillings a week in Nottingham, the conflict between his mother's ambitions and his father's dancing begins to take its toll. We are told that he was studying hard and growing serious, but "something seemed to be fretting him. Still he went out to the dances and the river parties" (54). Then when he is earning £120 a week and living in London away from his mother, William meets a girl at a dance and becomes engaged. The empty-headed "fribble" Lily, whom William nicknames "Gypsy" (perhaps a reference to Carmen), is his mother's antithesis. He writes to her then only "of the dances to which he went with his betrothed." When he brings Gypsy home at Christmas to meet the family, she talks about "London, about dances" (115, 117). William admits she is shallow but for "*some* things," he confesses he cannot do without her (131). The narrative winds up William's short life with a postscript. He had predicted to his mother that if he should die, Gypsy would quickly forget all about him. Two months after he does, Mrs. Morel receives a note from her stating: " I was at a ball last night. . . . I had every dance—did not sit out one" (141). With William dead, dancing is never mentioned again in the Morel household.

In the story "The White Stocking," dance is again the source of tension in a love triangle. The heroine, Elsie Whiston, a flighty, "pretty little thing . . . flicking her small, delightful limbs," is a modern Maenad (*Complete Short Stories* 1:244). Her stolid, middle-class husband, Ted, does not dance, but is the solid rock from which "she took [her] giddy little flights into nowhere" (1:250). Sam Adams, their former boss, is Pan to Elsie's nymph and their dancing together releases powerful forces, which, like George's polka dancing and Morel's sensual flame, cannot be managed socially.

The story is also triangular in structure. In part 1, we find out that Elsie has been receiving Valentine's Day gifts for the last two years from Adams, including a white stocking belonging to her, which she had mistaken for a handkerchief and carried in her purse the evening of Adams's Christmas ball. Part 2 is a flashback to that evening, in which Elsie, unmarried, accompanies Whiston, but dances almost every dance with Adams. Part 3 returns us to the present Valentine's day. Elsie puts on both white stockings and, in front of Whiston (to whom she is now married), dances "slowly round the room, kicking up her feet half reckless, half jeering in ballet-dancer's fashion" (1:261). Taunting him with her movements, Elsie becomes the first of several females in Lawrence's fiction to defy the male and dance her will to be separate. Whiston responds by knocking her down, and the story ends with one of Lawrence's ambiguous reconciliations.

"The White Stocking"'s publishing history, according to Keith Cushman, reveals the way dance crystallized in Lawrence's thought to become a significant part of his "metaphysic." The story was originally written in 1907 and revised three times over the next several years. For the final version of the story included in *The Prussian Officer* (1914), Lawrence changed Adams's character from "a rather gross old roué" to a dapper man of forty, exuding animal magnetism. He greatly expanded and intensified the dance scenes between Adams and Elsie as well (Cushman 155). These scenes prefigure the ones in Lawrence's mature fiction in several ways. The impersonality expressed in their dancing is linked to Lawrence's notion of phallic consciousness, or carnal knowledge. As Cushman says, the dance scenes "could easily be a description of sexual intercourse. . . . Adams does not speak to Elsie, and his eyes have 'nothing to do with her.' . . . In the dance Adams and Elsie have celebrated the cosmic energies of the universe together—but they have not attempted to know each other" (156).

While the story's naturalistic style belongs to an earlier period, a pattern of flood imagery in the description of their dancing connects the dance scenes in *The Rainbow* with the love scenes in *Lady Chatterley's Lover*. Dancing with Adams, Elsie is carried by "a kind of strong, warm flood" (*Complete Short Stories* 1:252). In their next dance, which is even more erotic, "Elsie seemed to swim out of contact with the room into . . . another denser element of him. . . . The room was . . . like an atmosphere, . . . under the sea" (1:254). In *The Rainbow*, Ursula, dancing with Skrebensky at her uncle's wedding, is carried away by "one great flood." The room "under the sea" in the story becomes in the novel a "vision of the underworld" (*R* 318). When Connie Chatterley reaches an orgasm with her gamekeeper, "it seemed she was like the sea, nothing but dark waves rising and heaving" (*LCL* 163). In all these instances, the image of liquefaction is a correlative for the mind's dissolving into the body through either dance or actual sex.

Dance Therapy: *The Rainbow* and *Women in Love*

In the earlier two novels, Lawrence found in dance a way to express the conflicts he saw between males and females, mothers and sons, society and nature, and mind and instincts. Reading Harrison's *Ancient Art and Ritual* in 1913 confirmed his belief that what is expressed in a dance is some greater inhuman will or realm of experience beyond personality and self.[5] Around the same time, Lawrence came into contact with Italian futurism, which convinced him that what the modern novel needed was a more impersonal, fluid conception of character than that of the "stable ego" handed down from the nineteenth-century. But before he could implement his new ideas about character or transform the nonverbal experience of dance into prose, Lawrence needed a more expressive style than the naturalistic one of his earlier fiction (we saw its partial development in "The White Stocking"). Besides a highly allusive pattern of imagery, Lawrence was also to devise a rhythmical, incantatory prose based on what he describes in the foreword to *Women in Love* as "the continual slightly modified repetition" (*Phx II* 276). The new language, the impersonal (or what Lawrence called "allotropic") view of character, and the emphasis on dance as a ritual in which one passed beyond "day-time" consciousness into the realm of the "Unknown" characterize the great dance scenes in *The Rainbow* (1915) and *Women in Love* (1920). No longer conditioned by their past, the characters are now responsible for redressing imbalances of love and power or reason and instinct, both within themselves and in their relations with others.

The Rainbow's three dance scenes—the corn-harvest pas de deux between Will and Anna Brangwen, Anna's naked solo while pregnant, and the moonlit *danse macabre* between Ursula and Skrebensky—illustrate how Lawrence adapted *Ancient Art and Ritual* and the futurists to his metaphysic. Harrison's thesis was that art and ritual arose from the same impulse: unsatisfied desire. Originally, art was purely a function of ritual and did not have independent status. Harrison tried to isolate the moment in the cultural development of Greece when the sacred dance of the vegetation cults ceased to be the "thing done" (dromenon) by the whole community and became instead drama and formal religion. When this happened, the community became the audience rather than the participants. Occasioning this separation was a combined loss of faith in the efficacy of ritual and the influx of a historically-oriented culture (Homer's Heroic Age), which put its faith in the power of the individual rather than in the collective energy of the group.

Lawrence rued the split between ritual and art. Instead of focusing on what was individual, he plunged deeper to evoke the nonhuman, unconscious bodily self within his characters, especially his females. Lawrence's desire to capture what is eternal and unchanging behind a woman's smile bears a remarkable resemblance to the morally indifferent blank stare on Yeats's dancer, who is "dead yet flesh and bone." But in the famous letter to Edward Garnett, written from Lerici, Italy, in 1914 while composing *The Rainbow*, Lawrence links his theory of impersonality to the chemical notion of allotropes and what futurists like Marinetti call the "physiology of matter."

> . . . that which is physic—nonhuman, in humanity, is more interesting to me than the old-fashioned human element—

which causes one to conceive a character in a certain moral scheme and make him consistent. . . . Because what is interesting in the laugh of the woman is the same as the binding of the molecules of steel or their action in heat: it is the inhuman will, call it physiology, or like Marinetti—physiology of matter, that fascinates me. I don't so much care about what the woman *feels*—in the ordinary usage of that word. That presumes an *ego* to feel with. I only care about what the woman *is*—what she IS—inhumanly, physiologically, materially—what she *is* as a phenomenon. . . .You mustn't look in my novel for the old stable *ego*—of the character. There is another *ego*, according to whose action the individual is unrecognizable, and passes through, as it were, allotropic states which it needs a deeper sense than any we've been used to exercise, to discover are states of the same single radically unchanged element. (Like as diamond and coal are the same pure single element of carbon). (*Letters* 2:281–82)

In *The Rainbow*'s first dance scene, Lawrence uncovers the "carbon" in his characters by replacing their proper names with pronouns and thus stripping them of individual identity. While they are courting, Anna and Will Brangwen engage in the simple activity of stacking corn sheaves. Their gestures, however, have a solemn, ceremonial quality and rhythmical pattern which feels more like a dance than a farmyard chore. According to A. M. Brandabur, this scene is analogous to the dromenon described in *Ancient Art and Ritual* (286). Their ritualized movements while harvesting are organically tied to the greater rhythmical cycles in nature. The hypnotic repetition of slightly modified phrases which describes their movements replicates in language the structures of creativity in nature.

But Anna at first is not so willing to surrender her ego, or "diamond," to become mere carbon. Instead, she tries to control the dance by keeping Will at a distance. "And always, she was gone before he came. As he came, she drew away, as he drew away, she came" (*R* 123). Gradually, the rhythm of their separate actions, conveyed in short sentences, modulates into longer, cumulative ones, which reach a crescendo when the couple meet face to face with their sheaves.

> And the whole rhythm *of him* beat *into his kisses,* and *still* he pursued her, *in his kisses,* and *still* she was not quite overcome. He wondered *over the moonlight on her nose! All the moonlight upon her, all the darkness within her! All the night in his arms,* darkness and shine, he possessed of it all! *All the night* for him now, to unfold, to venture within, *all the mystery* to be entered, *all the discovery* to be made [emphasis added]. (124)

One actually could dance to the highly alliterative, incremental repetitions of the slightly varied prepositional phrases in this passage.

The hint of an imbalance in their relationship is intensified in the next dance scene, where Anna is big with baby, dancing alone to Will's "nullification." "When there was no one to exult with, and the unsatisfied soul must dance and play, then one danced before the Unknown" (183). The Unknown is the life force or unknowable unconscious which is "by its nature, unanalyzable, undefinable, inconceivable" (*Fantasia* 15). Ideally, in a healthy marriage, the sexual act is a pas de deux into the Unknown. But Will's overweening need to possess and dominate Anna, together with her tendency, which we saw in the first dance, to insist on her separateness, cause Anna to sidestep her husband. Her ecstatic dancing transports her to this fourth, mystical dimension alone.

At first, Lawrence conveys Anna's dancing before her bedroom mirror on a Saturday afternoon as a positive celebration of fertility. Her movements are "fine," her limbs are "fine," and her face is "rapt and beautiful." Anna's swaying "like a full ear of corn, pale in the dusky afternoon" links this dance to the earlier one and its images of fertility (*R* 184). But when Anna realizes Will is watching, she repeats the dance: only this time she uses it as a means of dominating or controlling a fearful husband. To say Will overreacts to Anna's dancing would be an understatement. Like

Salomé, she renders him impotent with her dancing. He is "obliterated." Just the way the firelight bounces off her limbs makes him feel like "he was being burned alive . . . at the stake" (184).

It is not Salomé, however, who Anna harkens unto, but David dancing naked before the Lord.

> All the time she ran on by herself. She liked the story of David, who danced before the Lord, and uncovered himself exultingly. Why should he uncover himself to Michal, a common woman? He uncovered himself to the Lord. . . . Who was [Will], to come against her? No, he was not even the Philistine, the Giant. He was like Saul proclaiming his own kingship. (183)

In "The Crown," an essay written during *The Rainbow*'s gestation, Lawrence mentions David's "dancing naked before the Ark," to the exclusion of his spouse, "asserting the oneness, his own oneness, the one infinity, *himself*, the egoistic God, I AM" (*Phx II* 380). The Ark that David danced in front of was the "Womb" and "the darkness [which] builds up the warm shadow of the flesh in splendour and triumph, enclosing the light" (369). But David was "too feeble in sheer spirit" to conceive and remained sterile (380). Lawrence sees him as one of those warrior kings who "seek to pass beyond all relatedness, to become absolute in might and power," but deficient in love—"they fall inevitably" (380). Because he was imbalanced between flesh and spirit, power and love, David wore a crown of "sterile egotism" (380). For Lawrence, it takes two people in a dance of "pure relatedness" to achieve unity of being (373).

Anna shares David's "flesh" egotism because of the child in her womb. Lawrence implies that Anna would not have needed to dance or "exult" her pregnancy were it not for Will's imperfections. Nevertheless, without an adequate partner, her dancing, like David's, is ultimately narcissistic and leads to her own infertility of spirit. Like David, Anna will not dance beyond the threshold of the womb to be spiritually reborn in the Unknown. Like Moses, she stands forever looking out on Mount Pisgah, but is never permitted entrance into the Promised Land. But if "she were not the wayfarer to the unknown," the narrator tells us afterward, "still her doors opened under the arch of the rainbow" (*R* 196). Just as the covenant that God promised David passed on to David's son Solomon (who, being untainted by blood, was allowed to build Israel's Temple), so Ursula in the next generation will pass beyond the threshold of her mother's domestic contentment. After several futile attempts to find self-realization, Ursula will see a sign or promise of spiritual regeneration as a rainbow at the end of the novel.

But first, Ursula also must partake in a ritualized dance. Preceding her lesbian encounter with Winifred Inger and the forays into a "man's world . . . the world of daily work and duty" and higher education, Ursula has a passionate encounter with her lover Anton Skrebensky. When she is in her late teens (the same age as her mother during her courtship with Will), Ursula dances with Skrebensky at her Uncle Fred's wedding, in the same corn fields, under the same full harvest moon. Instead of initiating them into the mysteries of the Unknown, like her parents, the harvest dance proves sterile and destructive to Ursula and Skrebensky. In contrasting the two scenes, Lawrence charts the loss of efficacy in ritual which had occurred by Ursula's generation. Because the gulf had widened considerably between the intellect and instincts in this modern age, Ursula's dictatorial impulses are deeper and more repressed than her mother's. When they are released, her dance proves far more demonic as well as potent.

Ursula's dance also passes through two phases. In the first, which occurs at dusk, Ursula's repressed aggressive side rises to the surface, and her dance with Skrebensky becomes a tug of war between two resistant wills. "It was his will and her will . . . two wills locked in one motion, yet never fusing, never yielding one to the other" (318). In the second stage, she tries to suppress the male in Skrebensky. A full moon comes up and so do Ursula's autoerotic impulses. She offers herself to the moon, which in Lawrence's cosmology is female. "[Ursula] wanted the moon to fill in to her, she wanted more, more communion with the moon, consummation" (319). The language suggests a sexual union, but one which foreshadows Ursula's lesbian relationship and excludes Skrebensky. As Paul Rosenzweig notices, Ursula finds in the moon "an appropriate external correlative of herself and her needs, and she temporarily assumes the powerful qualities she has previously ascribed to the moon" (217). "She was cold and hard and compact of brilliance as the moon itself, and beyond him as the moonlight was beyond him" (*R* 320). Acting as the moon's agent, its cold light gives her the power of a "steel blade" with which she must destroy Skrebensky and the other party-goers who are "dross" and "loadstone" and weigh on her like "a blind, persistent, inert burden" (319).

Beyond its femaleness, the moon for Lawrence was "the centre of our terrestrial individuality in the cosmos. She is the declaration of our existence in separateness" (*Fantasia* 162). What Ursula emphatically expresses in her dance is a need to define her space as a separate individual. The need for "separateness" balanced with its antithesis—"relatedness"—is a Laurentian virtue, what Birkin calls "star polarity" in the next novel. But at this stage in Ursula's life, the need to remain separate is excessive and absolute, as the violent impulses released in her dancing testify. She wants to "destroy" Skrebensky.

> Looking at him, at his shadowy, unreal, wavering presence a sudden lust seized her, to lay hold of him and tear him and make him into nothing. Her hands and wrists felt immeasurably hard and strong, like blades. He waited there beside her like a shadow which she wanted to dissipate, destroy as the moon-light destroys a darkness, annihilate, have done with. (*R* 321)

Since Lawrence thought every individual comprised in different degrees both male and female, Ursula, in rejecting the male in Skrebensky, denies her own humanity. When she awakens from the trancelike conditions of the dance to ordinary "day consciousness," she is horrified by her behavior and attempts to "deny with all her might" her aggressiveness. "She was good, she was loving" (322). For the remaining novel, Ursula undergoes more nondance rituals, trying to redress the imbalance of antinomies within her. But she is not ready to surrender her personal ego to a third principle or force that transcends dualities until her relationship with Birkin in the novel's sequel.

Compared to *The Rainbow*, Lawrence's language in the three major dance scenes in *Women in Love* is not as exaggerated or expressionistic. Neither is the allotropic level of character Lawrence uncovers in the dance as elemental as it was in the former novel. The reason for this is fairly obvious. As Tony Pinkney observes, *The Rainbow*'s heavily repetitive and rhythmic prose mirrors the continuity of a culture (marriage, sex, birth, and death among the Brangwens) that is both settled and changing. *Women in Love* he sees by contrast as a synchronic rather than diachronic text. "*The Rainbow* is about a place that passes through time, whereas its successor is about a time that passes through places— the Midlands of the Brangwens, the London of the Pompadour café, the Alpine landscapes of the later chapters" (96). The characters in the latter novel are too highly aware of their complex, "modernist" experiences to be swept under by a prose that has "the inarticulate feel and stuff of unconscious process" (96). In short, if the characters in *The Rainbow* are carbon, the ones in its sequel are coal, or the next stage higher in the evolutionary process toward full self-consciousness.

Lawrence unifies the greater complexity of *Women in Love* with a structure that has, according to Mark Schorer, "a more immediate relationship to the art of dance than to the traditional art of fiction" (54).[6] Instead of a linear, temporal progression, the text, to use Lawrence's terms in the foreword, "pulsates to and fro" between the "shifting allegiances" (Schorer's phrase) among four major characters engaged in two frictional relationships: that between Ursula Brangwen and Rupert Birkin, which emerges out of conflict into the possibility of redemption through a new synthesis, and that between Gudrun (Ursula's sister) and Gerald Crich, which degenerates into a battle of dominance and possession and ends in death. Lawrence also presents the relations of the two sisters and the two men to each other. The shifting allegiances within the quartet are repeated and varied in relationships formed with minor characters.

The first dance scene, which occurs among the guests at Hermione Roddice's country estate, Breadalby, reveals both the characters' complex internal states and their intricate relationships with each other. As a counter to the endless talk or "rattle of artillery" about politics and sociology, Hermione insists on a dance to be executed in "the style of the Russian Ballet of Pavlova and Nijinsky" (*Women in Love* 84).[7] Gudrun and Ursula mime the biblical story of Naomi and Ruth, both figures of female vulnerability. We are tacitly reminded by Ursula's role as Naomi ("her men . . . dead," standing "alone in indomitable assertion, demanding nothing"), that she has just left Skrebensky in the former novel and has tried (not too successfully) to go it alone in a man's world (84). Gudrun, who plays the daughter-in-law Ruth, is fundamentally loyal but often jealous of her sister's self-sufficiency. As Keith Alldritt says, "[Gudrun's] outlook is conditioned above all by her propensity to disallow and thus thwart her responses and to withhold commitment" (166). In the dance her feelings of inadequacy come to the surface. She "clung with heavy, desperate passion to Ursula, yet smiled with subtle malevolence against her" (84). Perceiving Ursula's "dangerous helplessness," Hermione's anxiety that Ursula will steal Birkin's affections away from her is not unfounded. For Birkin sees in Ursula's dancing a "rich . . . dangerous power" and "a strange unconscious bud of powerful womanhood" (85). On the other hand, Gudrun's "female, subterranean recklessness and mockery," as Elsbree observes, arouses the battle instinct in Gerald, the same instinct which makes him both "coldly efficient in business and promiscuous in love" ("Lawrence" 21).

After the ballet, the two men reveal an essential contrast in their inner natures by joining the women in an improvisatory dance to Hungarian music. As the most conventional of the four major characters, Gerald's feet "could not yet escape from the waltz and the two-step," but he "was marvelously exhilarated at finding himself in motion . . . feeling his force stir along his limbs and his body, out of captivity" (*Women in Love* 85). Where Gerald's dancing is derivative but powerful, Birkin's is spontaneous: "a purely gay motion, which he had all to himself" (85). His dancing reveals a chameleon nature, capable (as Gerald is not) of breaking loose from the scheme of values imposed on him by his environment. Birkin will always go his own way in the novel, which is why Hermione watches him with impotent rage, hating him for his "power to escape, to exist, other than she did" (85). It is appropriate that Hermione, totally willful and incapable of acting upon her impulses, is the only one to abstain from dancing.

In the next dance scene, Gudrun practices her Dalcroze movements (eurythmics) on a shore while Ursula sings.[8] Lawrence, who was probably familiar with eurythmics through his German wife, Frieda, regarded Dalcroze's universal gestures, compared to ballet's highly stylized ones, as organically connected to a natural setting. Connie Chatterley, as we will see, performs her eurythmic movements in the rain in a denuded remnant of Sherwood Forest. But there is a mechanical quality to Gudrun's movements which goes against the grain of the vital force in nature. Beginning with some "pulsing and fluttering" gestures, she works herself up into the type of atavistic, convulsive movement reminiscent of Nijinsky's Dalcroze-inspired choreography for the dehumanized masses in *Le Sacre du printemps*. Ursula's "eyes laugh" watching her sister and at the same time flash a "yellow light," "as if she caught some of the unconscious ritualistic suggestion of the complex shuddering and waving and drifting of her sister's white form, that was clutched in pure, mindless, tossing rhythm" (157–58).

Like Ursula's in *The Rainbow*, Gudrun's dancing is a demonic release of pent up sexual and aggressive urges, revealing what she "IS as a phenomenon" and not according to a "certain moral scheme" (*Letters* 2:281–82). Eliseo Vivas classifies this dance as a "constitutive symbol," which he isolates in Lawrence as "a complex situation or scene . . . which gathers the significance of events preceding it and illumines the scenes or situations which follow." Yet he also sees its "self-contained intensity," which lends the scene the stature of an independent poem (Vivas 281). For example, Gudrun's dance "gathers the significance" of Hermione's ballet in that it dramatizes again Gudrun's jealousy over Ursula's self-sufficiency and her own feelings of emptiness. Gudrun begins her movements on the shore with the "desolating, agonized feeling that she was outside of life, an onlooker, whilst Ursula was a partaker" (157). But her attempt "to throw off some bond" with her dancing does not fill up the void or bring her any closer to life (158).

In the second phase, Gudrun dances perilously close to a herd of cattle that she spies. Their brute power both scares and arouses her. She confuses and stuns the cattle with her hypnotic movements, artistically manipulating them as elements in her dance fantasy. The dancing now becomes a "constitutive symbol" of an earlier scene in which Gudrun observed Gerald violently compel his horse at a railway crossing. The cattle, belonging to Gerald, are a synecdoche for his maleness.[9] Gudrun, jealous of Gerald's masculine will and his social/economic power, appropriates for herself his earlier aggressive behavior in brutally mistreating his horse. Gerald, hearing the cattle, rushes in and tries to stop her dance by insisting on the herd's danger. Gudrun, intoxicated by her violent gestures, responds by striking him in the face. Her act of dominance looks ahead or "illumines" the "final blow" to Gerald at the end of the novel.

The last dance, the *Schuhplattel,* an Alpine courtship dance, occurs late in the novel while the two couples holiday in the Tyrol. The dance is notable for "the extraordinary way the man snaps his fingers, slaps his thighs, buttocks, heels, knees and cheeks and claps his hands to achieve an extremely complex syncopated rhythm of sounds as he dances wildly in front of or around the girl" (Lawson 115). The man also emits wild yells and if he has strength enough, lifts his partner high over his head whenever the music reaches a crescendo. The male's imitating a cock during mating season is a vestige of the *Schuhplattel*'s origins as an animal dance.

The dance also signifies one last shifting of loyalties among

In Ken Russell's film adaptation of Lawrence's *Women in Love* (distributed by Brandywine Productions Limited, 1969), Gudrun (played by Glenda Jackson) performs her atavistic, eurythmic movements in front of Gerald's cattle. The dance, in releasing Gudrun's repressed sexual/aggressive urges and her need to dominate, reveals the impersonal "inhuman will" rising to the surface and displacing the "old stable ego" of character. *Courtesy of the Museum of Modern Art.*

the characters. Immediately following the bestial dance, Birkin takes Ursula up to their room to perform an unspecified sexual act that is new to her. Afterwards, Ursula reflects that degrading "things were real, with a different reality. . . . Why not be bestial and go the whole round of experience?" (*Women in Love* 403). Ursula's submitting to Birkin's "act of corruption" (which most critics agree is anal sex) signifies her growing trust of him and his ideas about "star equilibrium." Birkin is "self-responsible." His dancing and subsequent behavior, more than his fancy speeches, confirm to Ursula that authentic freedom comes from an untainted bodily awareness of the self through its physical rapport with another. After this episode, Ursula and Birkin mutually decide they have had enough of the sterile "snows of abstraction" and leave for a warmer climate.

During the *Schuhplattel*, Gudrun resolves to leave Gerald, and shortly after the dance she forms a new alliance with the rat-like German artist Loerke. Like Hermione earlier, Loerke is singled out by his nonparticipation in the dancing, since he, too, is a manipulative creature devoid of spontaneity and instinct. Loerke feels sulky and "pettish" sitting all by himself, since "he very much wanted to dance with Gudrun," and he jealously regards his youthful homosexual companion Leitner, who does dance with her (401). Gudrun next dances with a German professor, who, in reminding her of "a mature well-seasoned bull," connects her choice of partner to the earlier scene with Gerald's cattle. She cannot stand him "critically," but physically enjoys "being tossed up in the air, on his coarse, powerful impetus" (401). When Gudrun eyes Gerald dancing and exulting in his power over the professor's daughter, "as if she were a palpitating bird, a fluttering, flushing, bewildered creature," she is suddenly shocked with an "involuntary" insight into his character: Gerald was "naturally promiscuous" (403). Incapable of giving love, yet demanding and needy of sex, Gudrun realizes Gerald will always use women and bend them, like his horse, to his own will. Gudrun is hollow at the core and just as incapable of giving love, but she is a survivor who reads in Gerald's body language the warning that one of them "must triumph over the other" (403).

Pan Dancing:
The Plumed Serpent and *Lady Chatterley's Lover*

The destructive impulses that rise to the surface when the Brangwen women dance and reveal their allotropic states in *The Rainbow* and *Women in Love* are absent in the dances of Lawrence's last period.

Leaving behind a dead life and a dead marriage respectively, Kate Leslie and Connie Chatterley enter into the dance ritual with a burning desire to let go of their "old stable egos." Unlike the earlier heroines, Kate and Connie are conscious of the cause of their malaise, which is the ever-widening gulf between being and knowing that exists in the social order. Both go into the dance uttering the same oath: "Ye must be born again!" As a result, they achieve an immediate, mystical communion with the Unknown or "greater sex" and reach a further stage in the regenerative process. Where the earlier texts focused on the characters' relations to others and their own "essential" selves, the emphasis here is on dance's power to restore "the old broken impulse that connects [the individual] to the mystery of the cosmos again" (*The Plumed Serpent* 138).

To understand the pantheistic consciousness underlying the dances in these novels, it is instructive to turn briefly to Lawrence's essays on Native American dance rituals, written during the same period he composed *The Plumed Serpent*. In "Indians and Entertainment," he claims these dances are "the most stirring sight in the world" (*Mornings in Mexico* 50). When Native Americans dance, they participate in a natural wonder, not imitate it. So-called civilized peoples, by contrast, enjoy sitting in the theater like little gods, detached from the spectacle presented before them. However, the round dances of the Taos, according to Lawrence, are not spectacles because there are no spectators. Like the ancient Greeks described in Harrison's *Ancient Art and Ritual*, Native Americans do not distinguish between audience and participant. Even so, Lawrence admits that there is a big difference between Native American ceremonial dances and the Greek's early religious ceremony (51). Where the Greeks had some "specified deity . . . to whom the ceremony was offered" and who was the "essential audience of the play," Native Americans have "no conception of a defined God . . . But all is godly" (51–52).

In another essay, Lawrence connects this godliness with Pan, which he associates with primitive, elemental forces, both benign and malevolent (*Phx* 22–31). In pointing out the word "pan"'s etymology, Lawrence underlines the paradox in the ancient Greeks' transforming "that which is everything" into a concrete "grey-bearded and goat-legged" god associated with dancing and lust. Christians then translated the minor god Pan into a fallen devil with cloven hoofs, horns, and tail. Meanwhile, the "true" Pan, according to Lawrence, was alive and thriving in the New World. The aboriginal Americans experience the ineffable Pan all the time in their living relationships with trees, flowers, animals, the sun, moon, stars, and everything else in the cosmos.

In two other essays from *Mornings in Mexico,* Lawrence describes in detail two aboriginal American dances he witnessed firsthand while living in Taos, New Mexico, in 1924; of the two, the Hopi's "Snake Dance" is more interesting than the Santo Domingo's "Dance of the Sprouting Corn" (and will be treated in more detail here). Compared to Anna Pavlova's dancing with the Russian Ballet, Lawrence admits that the "Snake Dance" is nothing more than a "circus turn." Yet there is an underlying religious purpose to the monotonous foot-stamping and chanting among twelve priests of various ages who dance with rattlesnakes and pythons dangling from their mouths (62). As Lawrence's fictionalized characters dance to right an imbalance, the Hopis dance in order to put themselves into balance or "relation with the vast living convulsion of rain and thunder and sun" (65). Their dancing enacts a desire for greater potency from the powers that give life: the "dark, lurking, intense sun at the center of the earth . . . which you can no more pray to than you can pray to Electricity" (63, 65). By conquering their fear of the snakes, which live closer to the dark sun at the earth's center, the Hopis send them back into the ground with a message of tenderness and power. Modern peoples, according to Lawrence, conquered the dark sun, or "Dragon of the Cosmos," with scientific mechanical principles. Native Americans, on the other hand, seek conquest by "means of the mystic, living will that is in man" (65). Because our "gods [are] of the machine only," we no longer have famines, but a "subtle dragon stings us in the midst of plenty." Lacking a sense of awe in the universe, which the Hopis express in their dance, "the strange inward sun of life" fails us and "we die of ennui" (65).

Lawrence obviously had the Hopi's rituals in mind while writing *The Plumed Serpent*. Kate Leslie, a forty-year-old recent widow with grown children, turns her back on Europe for good, because she had been slowly dying of ennui and magic deprivation: "the dragon of degenerated or incomplete existence" (*The Plumed Serpent* 59). Despite some misgivings, she settles in Lake Sayula, Mexico, where she becomes involved with a radical social/religious movement to revive the ancient Aztec god Quetzalcoatl and rid revolution-torn 1920s Mexico of decadent Christianity. The communal dance around a drummer in "The Plaza," chapter 5, occurring shortly after Kate's move to Lake Sayula, signifies her individual redemption and serves a therapeutic function for the entire community.

Sitting in the plaza one Saturday evening, she sees a bonfire, hears the sound of a tomtom, and feels "that timeless, primeval passion of the prehistoric races," which she had also felt with the "Red Indians" in Arizona and New Mexico (117). The men of the Quetzalcoatl movement, wearing white *calzones*, red sashes, and ceremonial emblems, naked from the waist up, gather there to teach the peons the ancient ways of dancing. After chanting their hymns, the leaders began treading their "soft, bird-step" into the earth, revolving like a wheel around the drummer and fire. Then the peons and their women join in an outer ring wheeling in the opposite direction with the same "soft, down-sinking churning tread" (128). Kate, who wanted to remain out of "contact," is intuitively drawn into the dance. Holding the fingers of an anonymous peon, she forgets her individuality, race, and background and for a few brief moments becomes one with humanity. The creative power of the ritual illuminates the mystery she lacked in her old life. In the dance, she finds the life-affirming force of the procreative Pan.

Men and women alike danced with faces lowered and expressionless, abstract, gone in the deep absorption of men into the greater manhood, women into the great womanhood. It was sex, but the greater, not the lesser sex. (131)

In the last evocation of dance in Lawrence's fiction, Constance Chatterley undergoes a rain-soaked baptism in a bawdy eurythmic dance in Wragby Wood, her husband's ancestral estate and a remnant of the ancient Sherwood Forest. Like Kate Leslie's reawakening, the dance marks off a stage in Connie's regeneration through phallic consciousness, or her ineffable, sympathetic knowledge of and relationship to a vital, living universe. Her dance connects her to the cosmic rhythms the Hopis summon in their desire for rain and a plentiful harvest. It also marks a stage in her rejection of the sterile life of the mind represented by her husband, Sir Clifford, and his cronies at Wragby Hall, as well as the encroaching, ugly, mechanized world represented by the blighted Teversall collieries. The dance occurs in the novel's pastoral center, after her visit with the gamekeeper Mellors in his hut during a thunderstorm. While there, Mellors goes into a lengthy diatribe against the whole "modern lot"—workers as well as industrialists—who were "killing off the human thing and worshipping the mechanical thing" (*LCL* 203). Connie tries to dispel Mellors's despair by threading forget-me-nots into his pubic hair. After informing him of her plans to conceive his child, she has a "creative flash" and runs outside to celebrate in the rain her anticipated fertility.

> She slipped on her rubber shoes and ran out with a wild little laugh, holding up her breasts to the heavy rain and spreading her arms, and running blurred in the rain with the eurythmic dance-movements she had learned so long ago in Dresden. It was a strange pallid figure lifting and falling, bending so the rain beat and glistened on the full haunches, swaying up again and coming belly-forward through the rain, then stooping again so that only the full loins and buttocks were offered in a kind of homage towards him, repeating a wild obeisance. (*LCL* 207)

Stripping off his clothes, the gamekeeper follows suit. They make love on the sodden path, twine more flowers in each other's pubic hair, and perform a mock-heroic marriage between "John Thomas" and "Lady Jane," the gamekeeper's euphemisms for their sexual organs.

It is significant that the ritual elements of the chapter— Connie's eurythmic dance, the mock marriage, and the body-flowering—were added to the third and final version of *Lady Chatterley's Lover.* (In the first two versions, Connie merely runs through Wragby Wood with her lover trailing behind.) Lawrence intended to underscore his lifelong concern for humankind's reintegration with the life force in nature. In *"A Propos* of Lady Chatterley's Lover," he writes:

> We *must* get back into relation, vivid and nourishing relation to the cosmos and the universe. The way is through daily ritual, and the re-awakening. We *must* once more practice the ritual of dawn and noon and sunset, the ritual of the kindling fire and pouring water, the ritual of the first breath and the last. (*Phx II* 510)

This "means a return to ancient forms" from long before Plato, Buddha, and Jesus taught us "that the only happiness lay in abstracting oneself from life, the daily, yearly, seasonal life of birth and death and fruition, and in living in the 'immutable' or eternal spirit" (510–11). Writing to Connie in the final chapter of the novel, Mellors argues that the mass of men should "be forever pagan," that they should "learn to be naked and handsome" and "dance the old group dances" again, and that they should acknowledge "the great god Pan" as their "only god . . . forever" (*LCL* 281).

Lawrence is not advocating here a return to primitive ways. After describing an Apache dance ceremonial in another of his essays, he admits that he could not "live again the tribal mysteries [his] blood has lived long since: "My way is my own, old red father; I can't cluster at the drum any more" (*Phx* 99). But

Lawrence believed that by opening ourselves up to the spontaneous feel of nature's larger rhythms within our bodies, we could recapture through an imaginative experience the magical correspondences primitive people felt toward their universe, and as a result, a needed psychic rebirth.

Connie Chatterley is, finally, the apotheosis of all the women dancing alone in Lawrence's fiction. She is neither too cerebral like Lettie Beardsall nor too willful like Elsie Whiston, and Anna, Ursula, and Gudrun Brangwen. She does not need to dance out her defiance of the male. She resembles more Lawrence's evocation of the Etruscan lady pictured dancing on an ancient tomb in "Making Love to Music" who was "going gaily at it, after two-thousand-five hundred years . . . just dancing her very soul into existence" (*Phx* 166).

William Carlos Williams: "Only the Dance Is Sure"

*"A dance is a measured pace, as a
poem is a measured speech."*

Francis Bacon

"A poet should take his inspiration from the other arts too," William
Carlos Williams wrote Kay Boyle in 1932. After confessing a wan-
ing interest in Picasso, Williams brought up the subject of dance
(*SL* 133). The painters, after all, were not the only artists to influence Williams. He had been enthralled in his student days by Isadora
Duncan's dancing and was to enjoy a longtime, mutually produc-
tive relationship with Martha Graham. From the early imagistic
poems of the late 1910s to the variable foot experiments in the 1950s,
the dance is a prominent image in Williams's poetry, especially as a
figure for the imaginative process, which knits the disparate, broken
fragments of modern life into a luminous, fleeting wholeness.

Like the other three modernists, Williams saw the primitive
order in dance, which for him enables the isolated self to achieve
an identity by relating with people and things in the material world.
Dance is both form and motion, objective and intimate. According
to Joseph Riddel, it exists in Williams at a "pre-reflective" level of

consciousness, anterior to consciousness. The dance "takes place in a world of innocence, its form dictated not by a prescribed choreography but by improvisation stimulated by the response of the whole self to another or thing" ("Early Poetics" 55). Poetry, too, is the "form / of motion" for Williams, and what that form reveals is "the idea of the good in the intimacy of self and things" (57). The bad, on the other hand, is anyone or anything which alienates or divorces us from persons and things, like the Puritans, who denied their senses and cut off their relationship to the natural world by regarding its mysteries and miracles as signs of God's will.

Williams's dance figure is related to other frequently used topos, like sex, marriage, or the city, which also signify a gathering, flowering, or place where lines intersect and the disparate interpenetrates into the "white light of understanding" (Williams, *Selected Essays* 122). A man and a woman, say, come together in a dance, but the two do not melt into a Yeatsian Oneness, nor does their dancing tap something as exclusively sexual as Lawrence's phallic consciousness. Rather, their dancing, touching, or contact defines or discovers a third relationship or identity like Dr. Paterson's: "Say I am the locus / where two women meet" (III, i, 110; references to *Paterson* follow the form: book, section, line(s)). In the early imagist poems, Williams projects this geometric idea into concrete things, like the angle made by an attic or a ship's prow. Whenever he dances at the fulcrum of these triangular sites, his self-intoxication intensifies.

Williams's equation of poetry and dance as the "form / of motion" (*CP1* 339) has additional implications besides the ethical and epistemological. Just as dance creates a space of interacting forces emanating from the dancers' bodies, the poem for Williams consists of distinct but interrelated words or particles which interact with each other on a blank page like objects in an electromagnetic field.[1] Williams's words set down on the white space of a page behave like dancers drawing together and apart as they move through the blank space of a stage. J. Hillis Miller calls the visual relation between words in Williams's poetry "the juxtaposition of energies" (*Six Poets* 43). In other words the poem, like the dance, imitates (but never copies) the never ending movement and change which permeates the universe.

A 1953 poem entitled "The Artist" epitomizes Williams's attraction to the dance as a field of action or process rather than finished product.

> Mr. T
> bareheaded
>   in a soiled undershirt
> his hair standing out
>   on all sides
>   stood on his toes
> heels together
>   arms gracefully
>   for the moment
> curled above his head.
>   Then he whirled about
>   bounded
> into the air
>   and with an *entrechat*
>   perfectly achieved
> completed the figure.
>   My mother
>   taken by surprise
> where she sat
>   in her invalid's chair
>   was left speechless.
> Bravo! she cried at last
>   and clapped her hands.
>   The man's wife
> came from the kitchen:
>   What's going on here? she said.
>   But the show was over.

(*Pictures of Brueghel* 101)

For Williams, art is obviously not the thing made—for whatever figure the dancer makes vanishes even as he dances it—but the making itself. Mr. T, in his "soiled undershirt," is a far cry from Yeats's well-proportioned female dancer with the frozen smile. Where dance suggested a noun to Yeats, it functions more like a verb in Williams. As a late poem states:

> The dance! The verb detaches itself
> seeking to become articulate.

> (120)

The beauty of this verb is that it never quite manages to complete its action. It is forever "seeking," like those lovers on Keats's urn who remain forever young.

Williams himself loved to dance and claimed that were it not for his own gracelessness, he would have become a dancer. "Dancing is all the exercise my legs need," he wrote his parents from the University of Pennsylvania Medical School in 1904 (*SL* 5). He enjoyed watching professionals dance and often snatched time away from a hectic schedule to attend dance concerts in New York. Where Yeats and Eliot across the Atlantic were absorbed in Oriental dance and Russian ballet, Williams was particularly interested in the flowering of an indigenous art form—American modern dance. When he began his lifelong diatribe against transplanting European poetry on American soil, Isadora Duncan was already notorious for her outspoken, thorough denunciation of European ballet.

Williams's interest in dance ignited after watching Duncan perform in New York in 1908. He wrote his brother Ed that her performance caused his hair to "stand on end." Best of all, he continued, "she is an American, one of our own people, Bo, and I tell you I felt doubly strengthened in my desire and my determination to accomplish my part in our wonderful picture" (quoted, Breslin 31). Where Duncan rejected the ballet's stress on the musculature for a more organic movement emanating from the solar plexus, Williams would renounce learned literary conventions to return to

a *spontaneous* creative source from which these conventions originated. Where Duncan explored movement from the inside out,
Williams would attempt to get "the mind turned inside out in a
work of art" (*Imag* 75). Where other Americans were scandalized
by her scanty costumes and "immoral" life style, Williams rejoiced
at Duncan's rebuke of the Puritan strain in American culture. He
felt that her performance was "the most chaste, most perfect, most
absolutely inspiring exhibition" he had ever seen. In the same letter to Ed, Williams includes a sonnet addressed to Duncan that is
full of artificial "literary" diction and convoluted syntax ("your
deft step hath e'er conferred") obviously written before he discovered an American idiom closer to actual speech patterns. But
the last two lines are interesting for the way Williams confirms
Duncan's own Whitmanesque vision of America dancing:

> I saw, dear country-maid, how soon shall spring
> From this our native land great loveliness.
> (quoted, Breslin 31)

Years later, it was Williams's turn to inspire the dance movement through his conviction that "nothing is good save the new"
(*Imag* 21). American arts in general had to incessantly reinvent
their forms and languages. Trailblazers like Martha Graham in the
1920s began composing a radically freer language of movement,
which they reinvented with every new piece of choreography. Less
elusive than ballet, this new American dance descended deep into
the unconscious to express movement which was pedestrian and
plain, rather than beautiful and sublime.

But if his closer artistic affinities were with the burgeoning
modern dance movement, Williams remained open to other forms
of dancing as well. His attendance at a performance of Diaghilev's
Ballets Russes in New York in 1916 resulted in one of his most widely
read poems. Nijinsky's narcissistic, pagan faun in the ballet *L'Après-
midi d'un faune* inspired the image of the poet as a mythological
satyr dancing "naked, grotesquely" in front of his mirror in "Danse

Russe." Substituting his "north room," or attic, in Rutherford for the ballet's Greek pastoral setting, Williams weds the latter's "universal" connotations with a "local," mundane family drama. The "north room" was the busy doctor's retreat or sanctuary, a middle-class American version of Yeats's aristocratic tower at Ballyhee, in which Williams stole time away from a growing family and hectic practice to write poetry.

> If I when my wife is sleeping
> and the baby and Kathleen
> are sleeping
> and the sun is a flame-white disc
> in silken mists
> Above shining trees,—
> if I in my north room
> dance naked, grotesquely
> before my mirror
> waving my shirt round my head
> and singing softly to myself:
> "I am lonely, lonely.
> I was born to be lonely,
> I am best so!"
> If I admire my arms, my face,
> my shoulders, flanks, buttocks
> against the yellow drawn shades,—
>
> Who shall say I am not
> the happy genius of my household?
>
> (*CP1* 86–87)

When the speaker cries out from the attic's lofty height that he is "lonely," he celebrates the isolation an artist needs if he is to unify the demands of an inner, domestic world of sleeping wife, baby, and servant with the outer world beyond "the yellow drawn shades." Enclosed within the intimacy of his womb-like, triangular space, the poet's being expands outward. "Waving [his] shirt round [his] head," he apes the sun,

Nijinsky's narcissistic faun in the Ballets Russes production of *L'Après-midi d'un faune* (1912), the inspiration for Williams's satyr persona in "Danse Russe." *Courtesy of the Dance Collection, New York Public Library for Performing Arts, Astor, Lenox, and Tilden Foundations.*

> a flame-white disc
> in silken mists
> above shining trees,—

as life-giving center of the universe. By narcissistically admiring the movements of his "arms," "face," "shoulders, flanks, [and] buttocks" before a mirror, Williams's persona achieves a further sense of unity, in being both the creator and observer of his dance.

The differences between Williams's satyr and two other narcissistic dancers thus far examined are revealing. Yeats, in identifying with Mallarmé's Salomé, made an analogy between her inviolate, isolated virginity and his own art, which was separate and unrelated to anything in the world outside. The satyr's mirror, however, in representing or imitating the outer world, fuses life and art. To use Williams's terminology, his imagination is both whore and virgin to reality. In contrast, when Eliot's Narcissus regarded himself in the mirror, his body deconstructed into separate parts, which no amount of "clutching," "piercing," and "burning" could render whole again, ultimately causing him to turn his dance over to God, that most inscrutable of choreographers.

Williams's satyr, however, is the "happy genius" of his own ecstatic dance for several reasons. Unlike Narcissus, his dancing puts him harmoniously in touch with his real, sensuous nature. The speaker of "Danse Russe" is a satyr in the same sense that Aaron Burr was "immoral as a satyr" for going against the Puritan habit of "denying joy and maiming others." "The world is made to eat, not leave," Williams explains, "that the spirit may be full, not empty" (*In the American Grain* 205). Williams was to describe this condition again in *Kora in Hell* when he wrote: "Imperceptibly your self shakes free in all its brutal significance, feels its subtle power renewed" (*Imag* 68). The speaker in "Danse Russe" is also a genius in being an original, self-created talent, not one of those poets like Eliot or Pound, "content with the [literary] connotations of their masters" (*Imag* 24). In parodically echoing Nijinsky's mythological creature, the poet is also a genius in the sense of being the tutelary, pagan spirit of his place, his "north room," and his "household." And finally, punning on the word "genius," dancing in his triangular, hallowed site makes him a *genus* or point where all lines meet.

Williams also found a verbal analogue for the dance in this poem's rhythmical devices, especially its alliteration ("sun," "shining," "singing," "softly") and assonance ("baby," "Kathleen," "flanks," "face"). Despite the cosmopolitan title alluding to the Russian ballet in French, the form of "Danse Russe" is closer in spirit to the developing modern dance. Like the latter's break with ballet, Williams peels away the artifice of the English sonnet until it is a stripped-down, "barefoot" local version. Instead of the traditional sonnet's formal rhyme scheme, the unit of syntax "If I" initiates a series consisting of three conditional subordinate clauses. Then separated by a wide space, the traditional turn in thought or moral expressed in the concluding couplet is exchanged for a rhetorical question: "Who shall say I am not / the happy genius of my household?" Parodying the metaphysical sonnet's customary, artificial conceits of sighs and tears for an idealized beloved, "Danse Russe" becomes a self-reflective lyric celebrating self-love and self-expression. "We do not live in a sonnet world," Williams explained in a later essay (quoted, Cushman 104). So, unlike Pound, he would not teach "classic dancing" to "modern language" (*SL* 132).

Another early dance poem, "Ballet," has nothing directly to do with heavenly, ethereal sprites rising on their toes in *relevé* (*CP1* 92–93). The irony of the title rather reflects Williams's attitude about any kind of idealism that aspires "upwards," especially religion, Puritan striving, or the Protestant work ethic. Ascent is the direction of transcendence, but focusing on one direction alone leads to inertia, immobility, and finally death in this poem. This "lonely" speaker, gazing upwards, accuses a "great gold cross / shining in the wind" of being "weary" (lines 1–4) and "frozen with / a great lie" (lines 9–10) that renders it "rigid as a knight / on a marble coffin" (lines 12–13). Even a robin

> untwisting a song
> from the bare
> top-twigs,
>
> (lines 17–19)

is weary from laboring too much. The descent, we are reminded in a later poem, beckons, too. Passion, energy, and life itself come from the ground where we are in direct touch with our physical perceptions. The speaker implores the robin to come down from his winter perch to "the middle / of the roadway," where

> we will fling
> ourselves round
> with dust lilies
> till we are bound in
> their twining stems!
>
> (lines 31–37)

As Sherman Paul astutely notes, "Ballet" is in the shape of a dance or pirouette, which imitates the cyclical processes in nature. "The dance that [the speaker] imagines will bring in the day and the spring creates life out of the dust, out of death" (*Music of Survival* 69–70). "Ballet" imitates cyclical movement, or more precisely "twining," through continuous line enjambment, a term describing the syntax spilling over from one symmetrical quatrain to the next (a technical/visual device Williams often employed in his verse). One sentence, for example, continues through the above five lines without a pause at the line breaks.[2]

In "January Morning," the self merges with nature once again, this time as a result of dancing on a sea voyage (*CP1* 100–104). A young doctor "alone" is "dancing with happiness" enclosed within the protective, talismanic angle made by a ferry boat's prow, like the beams formed by the attic in "Danse Russe" and the intersecting lines of the cross in "Ballet." The poem is about a ferry trip Williams took home to New Jersey after apparently staying up all night on duty at a New York City hospital (Schmidt 65). Williams subtitled the poem "Suite" to account for the fifteen short stanzas composed of things he saw or imagined on his way home. The poem's cataloguing or naming of isolated, commonplace phenomena is figured in the young doctor's exuberant dancing and the forward motion of the prow; it releases the immanent power buried underneath the dead, winter surface of "curdy barnacles and broken ice crusts." As a result, the entire physical world is reanimated in the prow's wake: "Long, yellow rushes" bend, "gay shadows" drop, "exquisite brown waves" move, "the river breaks," and "the sky" comes down "lighter than tiny bubbles." At the birth of a new year, "against a smoky dawn," the poem celebrates a triumph over time in the endless cycle of death and rebirth in nature.

Williams included all of these dance poems in his third collection of poetry, *Al Que Quiere!* (1917). Significantly, he chose an image of some markings on a pebble for the book's cover because they reminded him of the figure of a dancer. "The effect of the dancer," he said years later, "was very important—a natural, completely individual pattern" (*I Wanted to Write* 18). The dance was "natural" because it was physical and earthy and therefore "imi-

tated" life. As an outward expression of subjective experience, it
was "completely individual"; no two people performed the same
movements alike.

Immediately following the publication of *Al Que Quiere!*,
Williams started working nightly on a book of improvisations that
would be published as *Kora in Hell* in 1920. He again emphasizes
dance and its source in the "ground," or local. The obsessive repetition of the word "dance" is associated with all that is creative,
liberating, fulfilling, and erotic. Dance is also mirrored stylistically
in the book's broken, exuberant prose rhythms. Section 15, for
example, begins with a verbal evocation of the dance: "'N! cha!
cha! cha!" (*Imag* 57). Linda Wagner-Martin also notices a dancelike rhythm in Williams's use of dashes and the "vertical spaces"
he leaves between words within a sentence, lending a visual tempo
to the line (21).

> Hey you, the dance! Squat.   Leap.
> Hips to the left. Chin—ha!—sideways!
>
> (*Imag* 56)
>
> So far away   August   green as it yet is.
>
> (34)

Kora also draws on the same dance imagery of earlier poems.
Like "Ballet" and "January Morning," the poet's frenzied,
Dionysian dancing expresses a lust for nature.

> . . . and I? must dance with the wind, make my own flakes,
> whistle a contrapuntal melody to my own fugue! Huzza
> then, this is the dance of the blue moss bank! Huzza then,
> this is the mazurka of the hollow log! Huzza then, this is the
> dance of rain in the cold trees. (34)

Besides dance, *Kora* shares with the earlier poems a related image
cluster of "toes, heels, tops, sides, soles," and plain feet. The shoes
on the decaying corpse of Jacob Louslinger in section 1 (either a
singer of or lingerer among lice), described as "twisted into incred-
ible lilies," repeat the speaker's dream motif in "Ballet" of rolling
on the ground with a robin "round / with dust lilies" till "the

pounding feet / of horses" would "crush forth / our laughter" (*Imag* 31; *CP1* 93–94). In "January Morning," the speaker's image of himself, taxed with overwork, discovered lying stiff and "staring up under" the "warped / bass-wood bottom" of his "chiffonnier," is related to the stiff Jacob Louslinger and the "stiff dance [of] a waking baby whose arms have been lying curled back above his head upon the pillow, making a flower" (*CP1* 103; *Imag* 73). In the dance of the imagination, winter and summer (or birth and death) pirouette together, making it impossible to differentiate one from the other.

The satyr also reappears in *Kora*. Although he is a more fully mythicized creature here than the happy fellow admiring his reflection from an attic mirror in Rutherford, New Jersey, he still represents, as Sherman Paul notes, the transformation of Williams's passion for things Greek into a passion for the local ("Early Poetics" 37). Williams describes him in section 16 as "a bare upstanding fellow whose thighs bulge with a zest for—say a zest!"

> He tries his arm. Flings a stone over the river. Scratches his bare back. Twirls his beard, laughs softly and stretches up his arms in a yawn—stops in the midst—looking! (*Imag* 60)

Kora, however, turns the dance imagery of the earlier poems into some new directions, which will be more fully choreographed in *Paterson*. The object of this satyr's desire, for instance, extends beyond the natural world and his narcissistic self. Why he "stops in the midst" and what he notices and pursues, we are told in the interpretation which follows, is "a white skinned dryad. The gaiety of his mood full of lustihood, even so, turns back with a mocking jibe" (60). The dryad the satyr/poet chases but never possesses is the Kora of the title. (Even Jacob Louslinger caught a brief glimpse of her "while bumming around the meadows": "Meadow flower! ha, mallow! at last I have you.") Kora constitutes all of the various incarnations of the female principle the poet searches for in hell. She is also the all-inclusive "Beautiful Thing" Williams would continue to quest after in *Paterson*. And finally, like Yeats and his antithetical dancer/mask, Kora is Williams's creative self and secret feminine nature—what Jung labels the *anima*.

Because Kora (Persephone in Greek) is so tied in to the meaning of dance in Williams's poetry, it is necessary to briefly note her genesis as myth. According to Sir James Frazer, who includes Kora among his "Spirits of the Corn," the young goddess was gathering flowers one day when Pluto, god of death ("the brutal lord of all"), raped her and carried her away to be his bride in the underworld (5: 1–34). Demeter, her mother, was so bereaved that she made the earth barren in her daughter's wake. Ron Loewinsohn interprets Kora as a "three-personed deity"—mother, maiden, and wife—who appears throughout the Improvisations in all of these guises. "As *Kore* (the Greek word) she is simply 'maiden.' . . . In hell she is the bride of Hades, above ground, the mother Demeter" (236).

Echoing the Greek myth, hell or winter in *Kora* is the ordinary world untouched or unexplored by the imagination and thus rendered cold and incomprehensible. The relentless movement which characterizes the twenty-seven improvisations—the burrowing, scraping, scratching, and digging—serves as an analogue for the poet's psychic descent into his own unconscious or the prereflective intuitive faculty Williams associates with the dance. "There's no dancing save in the head's dark," he tells us in *Kora;* that "which is known has value only by virtue of the dark" (*Imag* 66, 74). The plunge into the unconscious will result in a loosening of inhibitions; the speaker will be able to connect by creating "a new step" with his lady—"o' the dark side!" (67).

This new step, furthermore, will both uncover the uniqueness of "broken things"—"that peculiarity which gives an object a character by itself"—as well as connect the broken shards to each other because of that "one-thousandth part of a quality in common" (14). "Everything that varies a hair's breadth from another is an invitation to the dance," Williams writes elsewhere (*Doctor Stories* 89). The primal connection the dance makes for the speaker is between the music of the unconscious ("Hark! it is the music! . . .

Out of the ground?") and the words that make up a poem: "It is the music that dances but if there are words then there are two dancers, the words pirouetting with the music" (*Imag* 34, 32). The ideal dance the speaker envisions would be a slow one between the physical reality of things and their imaginative qualities:

> ... the wish would be to see not floating visions of unknown purport but the imaginative qualities of the actual things being perceived accompany their gross vision in a slow dance, interpreting as they go. (67)

Echoing Flaubert's famous simile likening the paucity of words to a bear dancing on a cracked kettle, the speaker learns by the second improvisation that words are clumsy and cannot always "pirouette" with the music. Often they inhibit the dance: "Again the words break [the musical rhythm] and we both come down flatfooted" (43). That language often betrays the dance is understandable, since the dance in its purest form is virtually untranslatable or ineffable. Like Mallarmé's *Idée*, the dance "is a thing in itself" (47).

The dance which connects the speaker to his fellow humans is not always a pleasurable one. The "stern dance" of disease (*Imag* 77) and poverty has taught him (to borrow a phrase from *Paterson*) to "embrace the foulness." When his patients' misery becomes too overwhelming ("an old man dying piecemeal," the "moaning and dull sobbing of infants"), he finds some relief by shaping it into a sadistic *danse macabre*, a dance of death rather than life. "Dance! Sing! Coil and uncoil! Whip yourselves about! Shout the deliverance!" (57). Similarly, in his story "Danse Pseudomacabre" (1920), the narrator/doctor characterizes the anguish of two sets of parents whose children die on consecutive nights as "an invitation to the dance":

> So, the next night, I enter another house. And so I repeat the trouble of writing that which I have already written, and so drag another human being from oblivion to serve my music. . . . Either dance or annihilation. (*Doctor Stories* 90)

More often, the Kora pattern connects the poet to the female sex: his wife as well as all the anonymous women, real or imagined. The naked women of the striptease, the young woman excelling at intellectual pursuits—all the living and dead, robust and sick, rich and poor, young and old—are aspects of Kora, or the Beautiful Thing of his quest. Women and dance are indissolubly mixed in the poet's mind with the imagination. Mozart's mind being so fertile, writes Williams, he "would whistle his own tune" and dance with his wife in the dead of winter. But when the speaker tries to write poetry, he is not nearly as agile or coordinated. For him, the process is like an aborted attempt at lovemaking or a clumsy pas de deux between himself and the object of his desire:

> The words of a thing twang and twitter to the gentle rock-
> ing of a highlaced boot and the silk above that . . . always she
> draws back and comes down upon the word flatfooted. . . .
> For a moment we—. . . . Again the words break it and we
> both come down flatfooted. (55)

Nor is the speaker always successful in partnering Kora in the glaring daylight of reality. So what he does is arrest her in an image of motionless dance:

> What a rhythm's here! One would say the body lay asleep
> and the dance escaped from the hair tips, the bleached fuzz
> that covers back and belly, shoulders, neck and forehead. The
> dance is diamantine over the sleeper who seems not to
> breathe! (47)

In the "diamantine," or diamondlike dance frozen out of time, the poet finds momentarily his "radiant gist," which was the goal of his descent and the aim of his poetry.

There is another dance going on in *Kora* which is equated with the figurative play of language. This dance demands a more active participation between reader and poet. To follow the dance of Williams's thoughts, we must play with his language at a deeper, less literal level than we are normally accustomed. In Freudian parlance, we must free associate till the images conjure up something buried in our own unconscious. Like a choreographer assembling dance phrases, Williams presents objects or motifs made out of language to the listener, but he will not manipulate our perceptions by interpreting them for us. In so doing, he intends us to get lost like his mother in the "Prologue," who always lost her bearings on the streets in Rome. The underlying principle behind both the dance and the improvisations is to "loosen the attention" and "see the thing itself without forethought or afterthought but with great intensity of perception" (*Imag* 8).

Interestingly, for all their opacity and subjectivity, the twenty-seven improvisations represent Williams's version of impersonality in art. In his "Death of the Author," Roland Barthes refers to the impersonality attained by automatic writing as the "desacrilization of the image of the Author." Automatic writing accomplishes this by "entrusting the hand with the task of writing as quickly as possible what the head itself is unaware of" and thus abruptly disappointing "expectations of meaning" for the reader (115). Like the enigmatic dancer and dance, Williams as Author only exists at the time of enunciation; he is born simultaneously with the text. Barthes would call Williams's writing of *Kora* a "performative" act, which like the ephemeral dance exists only in the "here and now" (116).

After *Kora,* Williams situates dance within the temporal framework of his revisionist history, *In the American Grain* (1925). In denying the New World the "pleasure of motion to release itself" (in dance or sex), the Puritans in Williams's eyes are the real villains of American history, and the "niggardliness of their damning tradition" is a "spiritually withering plague" (*In the American Grain* 130). "The May-Pole at Merry Mount" chapter, in particular, denounces the Puritans' malicious treatment of Thomas Morton for introducing a pagan symbol in the New World and "drinking and dancing about it for many days together" (79). Because the Puritans thwarted natural desires like dancing, according to Williams, they are the root of the perversions and violence endemic to the New World rather than our frontier heritage.

In the American Grain was also the catalyst for Williams's friendship with Martha Graham. Earlier, Lawrence had reviewed the work favorably, singling out its denunciation of the Puritans and its turning the genius of the continent into a mythic "woman with exquisite, super-subtle tenderness and recoiling cruelty" (*Phx* 334–36). Graham, likewise, responded to the book's evocation of female archetypes and its emphasis on sex as the single, great motivating principle in the universe. She wrote to Williams that his book marked a turning point in her career (*Autobiography* 236–37). Williams and Graham met earlier during her residence at Bennington College in Vermont, but according to the poet, "she was so closed about by the sheer physical necessities of her position that nothing had come of it," until he received her letter (237). At another point, Williams toyed with the idea of writing her biography (*SL* 171).[3] Shortly after the Spanish Civil War broke out, Williams and Graham—together with her photographer, Barbara Morgan—collaborated on a project intended to symbolize the horror of war. Morgan photographed Graham with a bomb exploding over her head and her body contracted into a spasm of mute terror. Delighted with the photo, Williams dedicated the poem "War the Destroyer" to Graham.

Williams also alludes to the dancer in a short story entitled "Inquest" (*The Farmers' Daughters* 317–21). An unidentified woman waiting for a bus prompts three inquests, or investigations, into the nature of feminine virtue, various flowers, and the differences between European and American dance. (Eschewing logic and conventional narrative, as it does conventional ballet, the story is a variation on Williams's female principle: flowers are women, women are dancers, dancers are "sexless" creatures who express sex by their dance.) The narrator calls Degas's dancers "ugly enough . . . from the American viewpoint . . . with their deformed legs. Dumpy little things." The Russians, "with their big peasant women" and the "leg muscles of Nijinsky" replaced the French (319). But all that "brainless classic ballet" is "peasant stuff" (320).

The dancer Martha Graham as part of a collaboration by Williams, Graham, and her photographer, Barbara Morgan, to symbolize the horror of war. *Copyright © 1941 Barbara Morgan, Martha Graham, "War Theme."*

> Now they fight against Martha Graham. But what else is there to do with the ballet except what she does? It can't keep repeating that saccharine putridity. . . . Each muscle is a thought—quite apart. Quite different from the conventional ballet. Martha doesn't grow old. (319)

After attending a performance by the Graham Company in New York in 1944, however, Williams detected a change in her choreography which went against his aesthetics and, incidentally, the principles that gave birth to modern dance. Less interested in articulating America than formerly, Graham began codifying her movement vocabulary and borrowing themes from English literature. In an unpublished letter to Horace Gregory, Williams accuses her of covering up a weakness of invention ("that distinction we seek anew with such great difficulty") with imported subject matter. He admits her premiere *Deaths and Entrances* is "powerful and impressive," but for all the wrong reasons. Graham loosely based her piece on the lives of the Brontë sisters. As it was neither "derived from our culture or our history," for Williams "its distinction came from the story," which was "a borrowed distinction."[4]

During the period he went to see the Graham Company, Williams was preoccupied with his own invention. By 1946 he had resumed writing poetry and published the first of *Paterson*'s five books.[5] Again, the dance functions like a verb in fusing or wedding the "virgin" "dream of the whole poem" to the "whore" of reality, with its "muck" and "bloody loam." The epic, in fact, is Williams's most ambitious use of dance as a reconciling figure, especially as it is embodied in his longtime persona of dancing satyr. The satyr image in *Paterson* is more impersonal and complex than its earlier metamorphosis in the lyric poetry and *Kora*. The frenzied dancing which ends *Paterson* book 5 (published ten years later in 1956) is modified or held in check by Williams's increasing concern for measure, which at this point in Williams's career had accrued new connotations.

At the start of *Paterson*, however, none of the dance's relatedness occurs. The inhabitants of the city "walk outside their bodies aimlessly / . . . locked and forgot in their desires" (I, i, 6). *Kora*'s ideal of a slow dance between "the imaginative qualities of actual things" and their "gross vision" is unrealized yet in the dance of the hero's thoughts:

> The vague accuracies of events dancing two
> and two with language which they
> forever surpass—
>
> (I, ii, 23)

But such "walking" and such "thoughts" create a rhythm that supports Williams's contention that the "dream [of beauty]" is "in pursuit!" (V, ii, 222). Williams, according to Benjamin Sankey, "means *[Paterson]* to appear not only as a completed design but as a recorded struggle—his own struggle to write the poem" (14). The aimless walking in book 2, the victorious hunt in book 5, plus the obsessive wandering and questing that characterize all five books concern fundamental rhythms related to dance, such as the beauty in the thrust and counterthrust of the river:

> . . . the river comes pouring in above the city
> and crashes from the edge of the gorge
> in a recoil of spray and rainbow mists—
>
> (I, i, 7)

Other rhythms capture the quiet, serene beauty in the movement of trees:

> The locust tree in the morning breeze
> outside her window
> where one branch moves
> quietly
> undulating
> upward and about and
> back and forth.
>
> (V, iii, 237)

Paterson also enlarges on the two counterpointed motifs in *Kora*. The Dionysus and Persephone archetypes, in fact, mirror *Paterson*'s structure. The Dionysian or male archetype traces a linear movement or progression *in* time, which grows increasingly violent and sexual in the first four books—like the apocalyptic "horny" fire that burned in Paterson's history in book 3 or the "shark, that snaps / at his own trailing guts" in "a sea of blood" in book 4. The Dionysian myth resonates most of all in the prose account of John Johnson, a hired hand who brutally killed his former employer and wife in 1850 and "was hung in full view of thousands who had gathered on Garrett Mountain in April . . . to witness the spectacle" (IV, iii, 203). (In one version of the myth, Dionysus dies a violent death by hanging and then is resurrected like Christ.) What gives the Johnson passage authority is its placement right before the conclusion of book 4, where the poet undergoes a symbolic death by drowning and is resurrected when his seed (or word) floats to shore and blossoms as *Paterson*, book 5.

The orderly restrain of the female principle, or Persephone pattern, curbs the Dionysian. It persists in the epic as a continuous descending and ascending movement, which links the seasonal cycles of nature with the death and rebirth of humankind in endless cycles or dances. Williams describes the process as:

> Persephone
> gone to hell, that hell could not keep with
> the advancing season of pity.
>
> (III, ii, 125)

Unlike *Kora,* hell is no longer exclusively confined to the poet's unconscious. Rather, it is objectified and repeatedly evoked: "Pursued by the whirlpool-mouths, the dog / descends toward Acheron" (III, iii, 132). Kora is more fleshed out as well. She is embodied in the newlywed Sarah Cumming, whose marriage to a false language drives her to a suicidal leap into the inarticulate roar of the Passaic Falls (I, i,14–15). She is also the Beautiful Thing as the black, gang-raped victim in book 3, whom Dr. Paterson calls on in her bedroom in the cellar. In her "white lace dress" and "high-heeled slippers," she reminds him of another ethereal creature, "the dying swan" (III, ii, 126), an allusion to the ballet Fokine created as a star vehicle for Anna Pavlova.

The poet also identifies with his Kora, or female principle, in *Paterson*. Adopting the persona of the nineteenth-century daredevil Sam Patch, he too leaps into the Falls like Sarah Cumming, because language fails him. He sees first "a sort of springtime / . . . within himself—ice bound" (I, iii, 36). For Patch, the "word" has not yet undergone a secular incarnation as it will for another persona, the lusty satyr of book 5. Patch's ironical leap and resurrection in the spring, "frozen in ice-cake," completes a circle and links the poet to the natural world. His leap into the Falls is also described as a kind of graceful ballet:

instead of descending with a plummet-like fall his body
wavered in the air—Speech had failed him. He was confused.
The word had been drained of its meaning.

(I, i, 17)

Paterson is also full of lingering traces of Persephone and
Dionysian dance rites, which once gave aesthetic meaning to life
and death.[6] While taking his Sunday walk in the park in book 2,
for example, the protagonist Paterson observes a group of immi-
grant Italian picnickers. Mary, a member of the group, sponta-
neously jumps up and acts out an ancient fertility dance in which
she resembles those Maenads who worshiped Dionysus. Mary

> —Lifts one arm holding the cymbals
> of her thoughts, cocks her old head
> and dances! raising her skirts:
> > La la la la!
> What a bunch of bums! Afraid somebody see
> > you? .
> > Blah!
> > > *Excrementi!*
> > —she spits.
> > > (II: i, 57)

The "vulgarity" of her dance is redeemed by the awakening of primal, atavistic memories in the woman's mind: "the cymbals /
her thoughts." Paterson attributes her intoxication to the "air of
the Midi / and the old cultures" of Europe with their pre-Christian
memories.

Mary's dance also evokes in the protagonist an image of a
slovenly satyr, aesthetically transfigured through the cinema.

> > Remember
> the peon in the lost
> Eisenstein film drinking
>
> from a wine-skin with the abandon
> of a horse drinking

so that it slopped down his chin?

down his neck, dribbling

over his shirt-front and down

onto his pants—laughing, toothless?

Heavenly man!

(II, i, 58)

Just as Mary's dance captures her vitality, Eisenstein's camera captures or frames the peon's Dionysian abandon in a way which belies his decrepitude. Likewise, the hero Paterson frames or shapes his memory of Eisenstein's image by intercutting or superimposing it between the two stanzas devoted to Mary's dance. In other words, he imaginatively "instructs" the "dance of his thoughts" (his memory of the film) on the outside world where Mary's dance occurs.

—the leg raised, verisimilitude

even to the coarse contours of the leg, the

bovine touch! The leer, the cave of it,

the female of it facing the male, the satyr—

(Priapus!)

with that lonely implication, goatherd

and goat, fertility, the attack, drunk,

cleansed.

(II, i, 58)

The scene imitates Eisensteinian montage with its abrupt juxtaposing of diverse spatial/temporal shots. At the same time, it successfully illustrates the aesthetic ideal elucidated in *Kora:* to see "the imaginative qualities of the actual things being perceived accompany their gross vision in a slow dance, interpreting as they go" (*Imag* 67).

Mary's undying dance also provides a context for the Dionysian letting go of the naked women dancing in the speakeasy (III, iii, 136), the dancing of the drunken whores in a Mexican brothel (V, i, 214), as well as the burlesque dance of the lesbians

Corydon and Phyllis (IV, i, 149). Most of all, Mary's dance anticipates the cathartic, satyric rites which end the epic.

The Persephone pattern, on the other hand, is reflected in
the more solemn dance imagery describing the Kinte Kaye, a primitive Native American death rite, which expressed continuity with
nature and the continuation of the community in the death and
resurrection of its king-father (III, i, 102; III, ii, 114; III, iii, 132).
Unlike the orgiastic gestures of the Dionysian dancers, this type
of dancing, performed in a circle, suggests a beneficent, shared
ritual. Williams implies, as Lawrence before him, that aboriginal
Americans through their dance rites maintained a sense of integration, which contrasts with the "divorce" between culture and
nature the Europeans made of their New World experiences.
Significantly, the white soldiers in the epic refuse the braves their
dance rites, just as the Puritans of *In the American Grain* outlaw
another communal rite celebrating the coming of spring, the
pagan dance around a maypole.

The progressive violence and endless cycles of death and
rebirth come to an end with the apotheosis of the poet into a dancing satyr in book 5. The satyr, like Yeats's dancing Shiva/Salomé
image, is an androgynous figure for the bisexual artist, who weds
both male and female principles in *Paterson*. As half-man and half-
goat, the satyr belongs generically to that ubiquitous group of
dwarfs, unicorns, centaurs, and other grotesque creatures of mixed
human-animal-divine attributes who dot the past and present,
mythological and real landscape of *Paterson*. As Dionysus' attendant, he fuses Williams's love of the classical with his insistence on
the local as the source of art.[7] When the satyr dances, "all deform-
ities take wing," just as Williams's creation of a new or authentic language raises the "deformed" or commonplace speech of Paterson's
denizens to a level of distinction (V, ii, 221).

The satyr's strategic position in book 5 also amends an earlier statement in the "Preface"

> For the beginning is assuredly
> the end—since we know nothing, pure

and simple, beyond

our own complexities.

(3)

With the last five lines of *Paterson,* Williams offers this cryptic qual-
ification:

> We know nothing and can know nothing
>
> but
>
> the dance, to dance to a measure
>
> contrapuntally,
>
> Satyrically, the tragic foot.
>
> (V, iii, 239)

The meaning of these lines do not imply a metaphysical position
like Yeats's illustration of unity of being through the undifferentiated dancer and dance. To "know" anything, even one's own identity, means to have experienced a relationship with some thing or
person(s) in the outside world. Like Lawrence, Williams felt it took
at least two to make a dance in his sense of the word. Knowing
through relation involves the imaginative act of imposing an order
or measure onto the random, chaotic facts of existence.

Because he associated dance with the birth of poetry, Williams
was fascinated with the measure underlying any kind of primitive
form—whether Native American dance rites like the Kinte Kaye,
the sacred dance rituals in honor of Dionysus at the Greek Spring
Festival, or those performed at the Eleusian Mysteries in honor of
Demeter and Persephone. In the 1917 essay "America, Whitman,
and the Art of Poetry," Williams writes, "the origin of our verse was
the dance—and even if it had not been the dance, the heart when
it is stirred has multiple beats, and verse at its most impassioned sets
the heart violently beating" (23). In a letter to John Thirlwall in
1955, Williams reiterates his belief that poetry traces its origins to
the formal arrangements in dance:

> Poetry began with measure, it began with the dance, whose
> divisions we have all but forgotten but are still known as mea-
> sures. Measures they were and we still speak of their minuter
> elements as feet. (*SL* 331)

Williams notion of primitive measure is about as elusive and difficult to pin down as his frequent evocation of a related concept called
on different occasions the "variable" foot, the "relatively stable"
foot, or the "new measure." The "old measure" he describes elsewhere as something "we feel but do not name" (*Selected Essays* 339).
In the final lines of *Paterson*, he informs us that the ancient satyric
measure is danced on "tragic" feet. However, an earlier passage
from book 5 links the satyrs with a "pre-tragic," or comic, beat.

> or the Satyrs, a
>
> pre-tragic play,
>
> a satyric play!
>
> All plays
>
> were satyric when they were most devout.
>
> Ribald as a Satyr!
>
> (V, ii, 221)

Joseph Riddel sees no apparent contradiction between tragic
and pretragic. For him, the satyr dance occurs "on the original
site where the pre-tragic steps into tragic, where the primordial
dance of form and power, or word and thing, broke off. It is the
point of departure of man into history, the place of blockage"
(*Inverted Bell* 35). For Riddel, the ancient satyric dance and the
"new measure" Williams seeks in *Paterson* are synonymous. They
are both characterized by absence and trace a lost plenitude. The
satyric dance, he explains, "precedes the word."

> It has no name. It is not a unity, but a dissonance. It is, there-
> fore, an opening a violent and inaugural beginning of the
> word which the word can never name. (40)

In *Paterson*, it expresses that which is ineffable, the "stream / that
has no language" (I, ii, 24). It is like that

> flower within a flower whose history
>
> (within the mind) crouching
>
> among the ferny rocks, laughs at the names
>
> by which they think to trap it. Escapes!
>
> (I, ii, 22)

If the satyr's dance is ultimately untranslatable as a "thing in itself," the image of his "tragic foot" is rich in verbal associations. With his cleft feet/goat legs, the satyr/poet suggests a defective, handicapped hero confronting a tragic world, one experiencing aftershock at the Holocaust and the ever-present threat of the atomic bomb. His dancing at the end of the epic suggests a way of coping with the horror, like the Jew

> in the pit
>
>   among his fellows
>
> when the indifferent chap
>
>   with the machine gun
>
>   was spraying the heap   .
>
> he had not yet been hit
>
>   but smiled
>
> comforting his companions   .
>
>   comforting
>
>   his companions.
>
>   (V, ii, 223)

Like Yeats's mask of "gaiety transfiguring dread" in "Lapis Lazuli," the Jew's smiling is an aesthetic gesture of order in the face of terror and a model for ordering our own lives.

Conversely, the poet/satyr has the dimensions of a tragic hero living in a limited, defective world. Paterson, New Jersey, in the mid-twentieth century is the antithesis of the heroic, Homeric age depicted in Greek tragedy. Where heroes like Agamemnon quest after ideals like family retribution ("tho' love seem to beget / only death in the old plays"; III, i, 106), we worship money in America, according to Williams, and crave the fantastic and exotic, imaged in the high divers, tightrope walkers, and whorehouses dotting *Paterson*'s landscape. In his parodic, "satyric" treatment of the epic, Williams is a satirist, and the new measure is more appropriately satiric than tragic in its mirroring modern absurdity.[8]

The measure which intervenes in the final lines of *Paterson*, however, is danced "contrapuntally" as well as "satyrically." As such, it resembles the dance in *Kora*, where the "trick" lies in "following now the words, allegro, now the contrary beat of the glossy leg" (*Imag* 55). The contrapuntal dance, in other words, harmonizes the satyr's tragic and pretragic feet. His tragic foot pulses with life's descending/ascending rhythms; his pretragic, or Bacchic, foot traces the wildly sensual rhythms of pure art. Since the satyr's dance weds the male and female principles in *Paterson*, it links sexual potency with the artistic imagination (Rosenthal 253).

On the other hand, the "Satyrs," from the passage beginning ". . . or the Satyrs, a / pre-tragic play," according to Emily Wallace, are not "the actual sylvan demi-gods who peer out of and between the lines in *Kora* and some of his early poems, not those shy, lusty creatures in pursuit of nymphs. These satyrs are mortals dressed as satyrs, professional actors performing on stage, innovators, creative artists." They are Williams's "tribute to the Dionysian spirit of the theater" (138–39). Wallace reads the entire passage from book 5 as an example of Williams's "concentrated form" in which he carefully avoids the scholarly controversy over whether tragedy—from a Greek word meaning "a chorus of goats"—evolved from satyr plays, which evolved from the dithyramb, originally a violent, leaping dance.[9] "Williams says simply 'a pre-tragic play, a satyric play!'" according to her, "because no one disputes that satyr plays existed before tragedies (and comedies)" (139). The pretragic satyrs are thus a concrete embodiment of Williams's interest in dance as the origin of verse. Aristotle, corroborating Williams's view, states in the *Poetics* that the iambic measure replaced the trochaic tetrameter, which was originally employed "when poetry was of the satyric order, and had greater affinities with dancing" (24). "All / plays were satyric when they were most devout" because they originated as passionate cathartic dancing, in which the participants felt within themselves the divine and creative attributes of their gods.

The final contrapuntal dance that straddles both the pretragic and tragic (or art and life) expresses in miniature *Paterson*'s collage structure. The new measure exists as new relations between words which have been wiped clean of familiar connotations and "rhythmically organized." In a fragment from a television interview with

Mike Wallace which follows the first satyr passage, Williams explains: "Anything is good material for poetry. Anything. I've said it time and time again" (V, ii, 225). Words rhythmically organized do not have to *mean* anything. The words in a poem function like those "dances of the Bacchic sort," which the Athenian stranger in Plato's *Laws* condemns as disorderly and frivolous since "all this sort of dancing cannot be rightly defined as having either a peaceful or a warlike character, or indeed as having any *meaning* whatsoever" (quoted, Wallace 139). *Paterson* presents to the reader examples of "found" language—like snatches of letters, newspaper clippings, advertisements, engineer reports, and such—which have been set down on the page to rhythmically counterpoint with literary language. The effect of spatially juxtaposing objects of art with artifacts from real life creates an element of ambiguity. This is the same kind of ambiguity created by the abstract shapes (art) of dancers' bodies (life) rhythmically interacting through space. *Paterson*'s collage structure, like *Kora*'s improvisatory one, requires that we dance with the juxtapositions at some elemental, preconscious level to be producers of meaning in the text.

After *Paterson,* Williams continued searching for the appropriate measure or form with which to articulate his poems as verbal dances. A heart attack, together with a series of crippling strokes in the 1950s, however, left him incapable of dancing with or of directly touching the objects of the sensory world. According to Carl Rapp, Williams withdrew "into himself to contemplate things from a distance." Instead of the things-in-themselves, Williams's thinking-about-things, or thought processes, became the subject of his poetry (123). In "The Desert Music" (1951), "The Dance" (1953), "Wedding Dance in the Open Air" (1959), and "Heel and Toe to the End" (1961), Williams's meditations center on dance. It remains, along with Kora or the female principle, his supreme figure for the artistic process. And though the satyr disappears, Williams created other "modern replicas" (to borrow a phrase from *Paterson*), who still remember traces of the old, primal Dionysian measure.

One of them, an ageing striptease dancer from "The Desert Music," is also another metamorphosis of Kora (*Pictures from Brueghel* 108–20). The poem, inextricably linked with Williams's recovery from his first stroke, follows the familiar *Kora* pattern of psychic descent and ascent (Mariani 631–32). A partially paralyzed poet journeys into the outer hell of an ambiguously fertile and vaguely menacing Mexican border town. At the same time, he descends into the inner hell of a shattered psyche which agonizes to achieve self-realization. The ascent "beckons" in a sleazy Mexican nightclub, where the speaker watches an "outworn stripper from the States." With "her bare / can waggling crazily," she "fits" an "insensate music" in the poet's mind, until then only "half heard" and "distant" in his memory. This figurative music is a "music of survival" since it projects an artistic order onto the fragments of reality. Later in the poem, when he conjures the stripper's image, things begin to connect for him. The garish colors of the Mexican marketplace and the "rank fertility" of the Mexicans are ameliorated in the "bright-colored candy" of the stripper's "nakedness" (*Pictures from Brueghel* 111, 113, 116). Like the old muse in "The Wanderer," who initiated or baptized a young Williams in the filthy Passaic, the stripper reaffirms to an ailing Williams that he is still a poet. She reawakens his senses. Her dancing enables him to poetically shape an earlier threatening image of a "form / propped motionless" on the international bridge between Juárez and El Paso (108–9). Before, the image of this lifeless lump had stuck in his mouth and rendered him poetically impotent. Now, its former connotations of death are reconciled with images from art and life.

> There it sat
> in the projecting angle of the bridge flange
> as I stood aghast and looked at it—
> in the half-light: shapeless or rather returned
> to its original shape, armless, legless,
> headless, packed like the pit of a fruit into

that obscure corner—or

a fish to swim against the stream—or
a child in the womb prepared to imitate life,
warding its life against
a birth of awful promise.   The music
guards it, a mucus, a film that surrounds it,
a benumbing ink that stains the
sea of our minds—to hold us off—shed
of a shape as close as it can get to no shape,
a music! a protecting music   .

                I am a poet! I

am.   I am.   I am a poet, I reaffirmed.

                (119–20)

The poet's private triangular shape from the early poems reappears as the "obscure corner" and "projecting angle," which Dr. Williams faced innumerable times before while delivering babies. Punning on the words "mucus" and "music," the earlier heard "protective music" becomes both the protective placenta out of which the poem is finally delivered and the amniotic fluid guarding the embryo "against / a birth of awful promise." Human life, like the poem, imitates the generative principle in nature, represented by the continuance of the fruit in its pit and the fish who swim upstream to mate and die. The "benumbing ink" in the pen which writes the poem is a stay ("to hold us off") from the shapelessness of death.

The next two poems move beyond the personal to explore the cosmic implications of dance. The elegiac lyric "The Dance" depicts a somber, Lear-like world likened to the "flurry of the storm / that holds us, / plays with us and discards us" (32–33). Fortunately, the dance intervenes and creates a chain linking various levels of reality. As snowflakes spin "intimately / two and two" as they descend to the ground, the finite self links with another as protection from the void outside. The mind dances with itself to keep out the cold by producing a work of art. As

Williams says, "only the dance is sure! / make it your own" (33). The barren reality of falling snow is imitated formally by the poem's minimal punctuation: three commas, an exclamation point, and a question mark. Enjambment directs the downward pull of our gaze on the page, which imitates the downward gravitational pull of all dance and life.

"Heel and Toe to the End," on the other hand, portrays Soviet cosmonaut Yuri Gagarin's literal defiance of gravity by dancing in outer space. Gagarin is related to other explorer/heroes of the poet's, like Columbus and DeSoto. But instead of a New World, Gagarin discovers the infinite possibilities of the old one, "one hundred eight minutes off / the surface of / the earth." Even from that mind-boggling, dizzying height, a measure intervenes, as it did in *Paterson* and "The Desert Music." This measure is also relational. For Gagarin, it is a scientific, Einsteinian measure ("all that division and / subtraction") which brings him safely back to earth. For the poet, it is an aesthetic or imaginative measure which orders and shapes reality, grounded in the foot and the ancient "divisions" of dance:

> from all that division and
> subtraction a measure
> toe and heel
>
> heel and toe he felt
> as if he had
> been dancing.

(69)

Postscript

From Yeats's ethereal faeries, to Eliot's self-flagellating saint, and finally Williams's earthy stripper, the years covered in this study brought several changes in the modernist dancer. Underlining the variety are distinct notions about what dance is or should be, which in turn, are indicative of larger ideological differences.

Eliot's literary and spiritual sensibilities, for example, drew him to classical ballet. Its verticality and highly specialized technique constituted the control, refinement, and transcendence of the body through the mastery of learned, prescribed choreography. His conservatism found a congenial mirror in a ballet company's authoritarian, hierarchical structure, its unified point of view, the rigorous training of its cloistered members, and most of all, its role as a transmitter of tradition in which past ballets were handed down to and reinvented by every generation.

Unacquainted and uninterested in professional dancers, Lawrence dwells on the importance of dance in everyday life rather than art. His variety of dance is instinctual, natural, and improvised, an efficacious activity for every member in society. After reading Harrison's *Ancient Art and Ritual,* Lawrence also became excited about the ancients feeling attuned or unified with their external world through dance. But instead of wanting to recapture this unity for the theater like Eliot, Lawrence planned that daily communal dancing would play an integral part in Rananim, his unrealized Utopia (Boulton 951).

Williams, like Lawrence, looked at dance as a cathartic "letting go" and freeing of the body. In contrast to Eliot, he came to see ballet's "brainless" repetition as obsolete and foreign to American soil. Williams's own poetic of "nothing is good save the new" is mirrored in the early modern dance movement in America. The new dance, like Williams's poetry, had its roots in the local and probed the unconscious for a plainer, less stylized movement vocabulary. Instead of ballet's heavenly ascent, it hugged the life-sustaining ground.

Yeats, the eclectic Celt, embraced all forms of dance. The particular backgrounds of his dancer/collaborators—eurythmic-trained Michio Ito and ballet-trained Ninette de Valois—were irrelevant, since he equally covered them up with masks. Yeats, moreover, was drawn to the Oriental themes of two stylistically antithetical soloists: Ruth St. Denis and Anna Pavlova. Yet his greatest artistic affinities were with Loïe Fuller's symbolist art.

Despite their differences, the influence of dance on their collective works enlarges our understanding of high modernism as a period of revolutionary vision. For both the fierce asceticism of the period and the deep nostalgia for an earlier age are apparent in their attraction to dance. They saw that the substance of dance, its primitive wholeness, harked back to a simpler, less fragmented time than their own. Yet they also saw that the form of the dance, its impersonality, was modern.

To all four, both dancer and dance are intimately bound up with modernism's language experiments. All four strove to capture dance rhythms in their verse and prose. Repeatedly, the dance's more abstract semiosis—its looser correspondence between signifier and signified—serves as a model in freeing the poem or narrative from too narrow and literal a meaning. The dances in Eliot's "Burnt Norton," Yeats's "Byzantium," and Lawrence's *The Rainbow,* for example, signal a wave of rhetorical devices which dance or play around a missing center. Similarly, the dance's improvisatory nature serves as a method through which Williams continuously thwarts the reader's expectations of meaning in *Kora in Hell.*

In addition, all four modernists see dance occurring at some unconscious level and signifying some deeply felt experience which eludes verbal utterance. Yeats felt dance's trancelike rhythms raise or alter daytime consciousness into a twilight realm between sleeping and awaking. In "Byzantium," dance enables the soul to transcend the wheel of endless reincarnations. Being swept up into the rhythms of a collective dance allows the speaker to forget his isolation as an "old scarecrow." Eliot felt dance rhythms travel to the brain through the neurological system (the "dance along the arteries") and evoke the spiritual by tapping latent religious archetypes residing in the psychological unconscious. Lawrence also felt that dance is experienced in the blood (moving in the opposite direction) and that it constitutes phallic consciousness, or man's sympathetic, intuitive awareness of all living things. Williams, finally, envisions dance as a numinous, prereflective state anterior to language, which is capable of loosening the mind of its inhibitions. He calls dance "the thing-in-itself," while Eliot labels it the "still point." Eliot concludes "there is only the dance," while Williams confirms that "only the dance is sure." To Lawrence, dance recovers the sense of awe and mystery missing in the modern age, and to Eliot, it simplifies "current life into something rich and strange."

Yet the cross-fertilization between dance and literary modernism does not end here. The vectors of influence traveled the other way as well. Ruth St. Denis and Ted Shawn (her partner/ husband) as well as Martha Graham were, like Lawrence, deeply inspired by the ecstatic dance rituals of aboriginal Americans. At her request, Graham's ashes were dispersed in the New Mexican desert, as were Lawrence's fifty years earlier. What is more important, Graham's symbolist dance theater and her collaborations with Japanese sculptor Isamu Noguchi drew on the expressionistic style of Yeats's Noh plays. Significantly, Graham based her version of the Salomé myth, *Hérodiade,* on Mallarmé's poem (rather than Wilde's play); the icy, narcissistic dancer fixated by her reflection in Noguchi's mirror is akin to the image with which Yeats identifies in his essays. Moreover, Graham's reading of Williams's *In the American Grain* inspired the archetypal American heroines of *Frontier, American Provincials,* and *American Document. Paterson*'s rightful heir, however, is Merce Cunningham, a former Graham Company member and representative of the third generation of modern choreographers. Like the mix of art and life language in Williams's epic, Cunningham's choreography juxtaposes pedestrian (nondance) movement with stylized gestures and plays with dance conventions to thwart audiences' expectations of meaning. And even Old Possum left his imprint on the dance world, when his *Book of Practical Cats* and a segment of the poem "Rhapsody on a Windy Night" were transformed into the exuberant feline dancing of Andrew Lloyd Weber's musical *Cats.*

Notes

Introduction

1. Monroe Spears's *Dionysus and the City,* for example, focuses on parallel developments in the arts during the modernist era, including Schöenberg's atonal music, but fails to mention any of the choreographers involved with the new dance.

For the handful of intertextual studies on modernism and dance, the reader is referred to: Frank Kermode, *Romantic Image,* and his essay "Poet and Dancer before Diaghilev"; Audrey Rodgers, *The Universal Drum: Dance Imagery in the Poetry of Crane, Eliot, Roethke, and Williams;* Langdon Elsbree, "D. H. Lawrence, Homo Ludens, and the Dance"; and David Bernstein, "Dance in the *Four Quartets."*

2. In the Western theatrical tradition, dance has been closely associated with the female body. In the nineteenth-century Romantic era especially (when Marie Taglioni first donned toe shoes and elevated herself in *La Sylphide*), the ballerina, following the dictates of male choreographers, transcended her body or matter to become "pedestalized" into an ethereal sprite. The *danseur,* moreover, was little more than a porter who moved the ballerina around the stage, enabling her to accomplish acrobatic feats while balanced on one leg *en pointe.*

In contrast, the precursors of the modern dance movement in the early part of the twentieth-century—soloists Loïe Fuller, Isadora Duncan, Ruth St. Denis, and Maud Allan—created images out of their own unballetic bodies. The next generation of dancers in the 1930s, like Mary Wigman, Martha Graham, and Doris Humphrey, controlled their own companies and created an entirely new movement vocabulary, which often utilized the ground or gravity.

3. Jaques-Dalcroze sent Diaghilev one his most promising students, a young Polish woman named Marie Rambert, to be Nijinsky's assistant. Rambert, along with Ninette de Valois, eventually became a founder of the British ballet (Rambert 55–71).

4. Fokine was one of the great reformers of ballet. When Diaghilev assembled a troupe of Russian dancers for a Paris season in 1909, he hired

Notes

Fokine as his chief choreographer. Western audiences were thus the first to see the choreographer's ideas put into practice. Basically, Fokine created a more expressive, organic form of movement based on the dramatic situation, the time, and the character of the music instead of relying on already fixed steps. Ancient Egyptians, medieval Arabs, and Tartars simply did not move in tutus, toe shoes, and the five, turned-out leg positions prescribed in the aristocratic courts of sixteenth-century France. Fokine also broke tradition by choreographing more equally featured movements for men and women. He did away with artificial conventions like the traditional *divertissements* of the corps de ballet, which previously functioned as mere decorative flourish. His movements for large groups of dancers moving in wavelike patterns on and off the stage were logically tied to the dramatic action.

5. Sandra M. Gilbert and Susan Gubar interpret "male-defined" modernism's preoccupation with the *femme fatale* (especially in Yeats) as a "recuperative strategy" or attempt to "reconstitute a shattered *patrius sermo*" (3–46).

6. *L'Après-midi d'un faune* (1912) was loosely based on the Mallarmé poem in which a faun sees or imagines a group of nymphs in the distance. He pursues them, looses them, and then relives the memory of lust and frustrated desire. The last image is a startling masturbatory one in which the faun makes an amorous descent on the scarf left behind by the chief nymph. *Jeux* (1913) was a *ménage à trois* for two women and a man which explored ambiguous sexual relations under the guise or metaphor of sport. Nijinsky, according to Arlene Croce, made "the relation between the dancer's sexuality and the dancer's art absolute. . . . If the trilogy of *Faune, Jeux* and *Sacre* has any biographical meaning at all, it is a biography of the orgasm: at first self-induced, later consciously manipulated through the piquancy and perversity of intimate relations, and finally a vast and sweated communal seizure, with death and life occurring together in a shattering rhythm" (267).

7. As Deborah Jowitt notes, Fuller was not an isolated phenomenon in dance. Like the choreographer, Alwin Nikolais, and the dance companies, Pilobolus and Mummenschanz, she belonged to a tradition in dance which conceals and transforms the body into metaphor, as opposed to another like Balanchine's, which sublimates the female form into an etherialized spirituality (341–73).

8. Eliot, "London Letter," *Dial* (July 1921).

9. Wagner had argued earlier that poetry and music should cooperate with the arts of the theater to produce new compound forms which would be higher and greater than any of these arts in isolation.

W. B. Yeats

1. Ito staged *At the Hawk's Well* twice in the United States: New York in 1918 and California in 1929. In 1939 he translated the play into Japanese and performed it in Japan, where it was regarded as a genuine Noh play and made part of the country's permanent Noh repertory.

2. According to Donne, Elizabeth Drury's

> pure and eloquent blood
> Spoke in her cheekes, and so distinctly wrought,
> That one might say, her body thought.
> (*Second Anniversary* section 2, lines 244–46)

3. In the first Noh-inspired dance play, *At the Hawk's Well* (1916), the Salomé image is presented at several removes; the young Cuchulain is cursed for his dealings with the dancers or women of the Sidhe. In three later dance plays, *A Full Moon in March* (1935), *The King of the Great Clock Tower* (1935), and *The Death of Cuchulain* (1937), the Salomé image is made explicit. In the first, a queen dances before the severed head of a swineherd/singer which she places on the throne; in the second, another queen ("wearing a beautiful impassive mask") dances with the severed head of the king placed on her shoulders. In the last play (and Yeats's final word on the dancer), Emer, Cuchulain's wife, dances before his severed head, which instead of a mask is featured as a plain black parallelogram.

In his notes to *The King of the Great Clock Tower* (1935), Yeats admitted borrowing the dance of the severed head from Wilde, who borrowed it from Heinrich Heine, who probably found it in some Jewish religious legend. Yeats then linked the image to a universal vegetation myth or "ritual of the year: the mother goddess and the slain god" (*Variorum Plays* 1010).

4. Jowitt notes how Salomés "executed their grisly movements" at opera houses, vaudeville stages, and the movies. Diaghilev produced *Salomé* in 1913, starring Tamara Karsavina with choreography by Boris Romanov and Beardsley-like decor by Serge Soudeikine. Loïe Fuller's *La Tragédie de Salomé* in 1907 was a fusion of turbulent lighting effects on a series of solos, which included her dancing in peacock feathers and playing with two six-foot snakes (111). After turning down repeated offers to dance the role in Oscar Wilde's play in 1907, the more spiritual, idealistic St. Denis finally consented and staged and performed her own *Salomé* in 1931.

162   Even if Yeats had not seen the above performances, he was probably familiar with the French treatment of the legendary dancer through Flaubert's *Salammbo,* Gautier's *Clarimonde,* and the misty, glittering Salomé paintings of Gustave Moreau. It is also likely he knew Gustav Klimt's imperturbable and gilded *Salomé* and his *Judith* with the head of Holofernes—dancers did not have the image patented.

5. Shiva's right earring is a man's; the left earring, a woman's. The god's statue is made up of both a vertical stone shaft and a female, circular horizontal base called a "yoni" or "pitha" (Hanna 110).

6. The first manuscript copy of "The Hosting of the Sidhe" is dated 1893 (Bradford 19).

7. Robartes is a character who escaped from Yeats's earlier short stories and reappears in *A Vision* along with Owen Aherne (Jeffares, *A New Commentary* 49).

8. This is only one reading of the dancer in "Double Vision." Along with the Sphinx and Buddha, she has inspired differing critical interpretations. For Unterecker, she is a symbol of "order in a partly disordered world"; specifically, "the supersensual equivalent of mundane ordered things, the image which the artist—seeking form—copies, the vision which both inspires and justifies him" (*Reader's Guide to Yeats* 156). Ellmann calls the Sphinx the intellect, the Buddha the heart, and the dancing girl "primarily an image of art." "She dances between them because art is neither intellectual nor emotional but a balance of these qualities" (255–56). Bloom, who analyzes the poem in Shelleyean and Blakean terms, concludes that the Sphinx is "knowledge without love," the Buddha "love without knowledge," and the dancing girl sandwiched in between celebrates "the mystery of incarnate beauty, the triumph of art in Phase 15" (207). Finally Kermode, who bases his interpretation on Yeats's statements in *A Vision,* identifies the Sphinx as the "introspective knowledge of the mind's self-begotten unity," the subjective or antithetical; the Buddha as "the outward-looking mind," the objective or primary; and the girl as achieved unity of being or complete subjectivity, which Kermode describes as "the miraculous moment of perfection beyond nature, revelation" (*Romantic Image* 59).

9. In a letter written to Olivia Shakespear in 1926, Yeats described the poem as his "last curse on old age." In one of the drafts, he attached a note saying : "Bring in the old thought that life prepares for what never happens" (quoted, Jeffares, *A New Commentary* 251, 253).

10. See especially Brooks 178–91, Wain 194–210, and Kermode, *Romantic Image* 85–86.

11. There is a debate in dance theory which undermines de Man's assumption that the final two lines are generally read as a rhetorical question. Dance theorists like Nelson Goodman would respond quite literally to Yeats's query about differentiating the dancer from the dance. Yeats could have been raising an aesthetic issue: namely, how much does a dancer bring of his or her personal, expressive style (either consciously or unconsciously) to the choreography? Is *La Spectre de la rose,* for example, the same ballet without Nijinsky's inimitable leap? In other words, is dance *autographic* (in the sense that the most exact duplication will not count as genuine) or *allographic* (in the sense that it can be replicated by a notational system, independent of the history of production)? For an expanded discussion of this issue, see Goodman, 399–410.

12. For an expanded account of Yeats's relationship to Susan Pollexfen Yeats, see Lynch, *Yeats: The Poetics of the Self.* Lynch interprets several of the major poems in light of Yeats's narcissism, which he sees resulting from Susan Yeats's withheld love during a crucial stage in the poet's early development.

13. George Melchiori has drawn attention to the fire dance's similarity with another dance ending in a trance in the short story "Rosa Alchemica" published in 1896. The story describes the occult, alchemical rituals of an esoteric sect, like the Golden Dawn to which Yeats belonged at the time. Michael Robartes takes the narrator to a "great circular room" in which the latter engages in an increasingly passionate dance with mortals partnering immortals ("I was able to distinguish beautiful Grecian faces and august Egyptian faces") and then falls into a swoon. Afterward, he is told by Robartes that the purpose of the dance was so "the gods may make them [the immortals] bodies out of the substance of our hearts" (*Mythologies* 289). The dance, like the one in "Byzantium," is part of "a universal transmutation of all things into some divine and imperishable substance" (270).

14. See also "Leda and the Swan," "A Woman Homer Sung," "When Helen Lived," and "Three Marching Songs" in the *Collected Poems.*

T. S. Eliot

1. In 1958, after Eliot married his second wife, Valerie Fletcher, and brought her to Harvard, he confessed to some Cambridge reporters that he might take dancing lessons again as "I have not danced at all for some

Notes

years." The Eliots, in fact, were the only "adults" among the invited faculty and their guests to make an appearance at a late-night undergraduate ball (Gordon, *New Life* 256).

2. Pound alluded to Eliot's portrait of Astafieva in his *Pisan Cantos.*

> Grishkin's photo refound years after
> with the feeling that Mr. Eliot may have
> missed something, after all, in composing his vignette.
>
> (canto 78, lines 73–75)

In contrast to Eliot, Pound commended her as a transmitter of the ancient tradition of dance.

> So Astafieva had conserved the tradition
> From Byzance and before then.
>
> (canto 79, lines 178–79)

3. "Narcissus" was among the many verses Eliot had originally planned to include in *The Waste Land* that Pound either cut or radically revised. Eventually, the prophet/dancer evolved into a larger, more impersonal work as the prophetic voice in the desert in lines 26–30 of "The Burial of the Dead" section. This voice invites the reader to "Come in under the shadow of this red rock," and experience the shadow as "fear in a handful of dust" (*SP* 51–52). An androgynous figure capable of expressing simultaneous points of view, Narcissus became the prototype of the prophet Tiresias. The final image of his dryness—"the shadow in his mouth"—became, of course, one of the poem's major motifs.

4. In addition to the Greek myth, Narcissus conflates several other sources. Lyndall Gordon suggests Eliot drew on the following religious models: the second century Bishop of Jerusalem who hid in the desert for several years, Saint Augustine and his trials in Carthage, and Saint Sebastian who suffered martyrdom at the hands of archers (*Early Years* 91). Other critics have suggested literary echoes from Hulme's "Conversion" and Herbert's "Affliction." Mayer thinks Eliot based the character on Paul Valéry, a poet whom he respected and of whom he wrote: "he reminds us of Narcissus gazing into the pool, and partakes of the same attraction and the mystery of Narcissus, the aloofness and frigidity of that spiritual celibate" (quoted, Mayer 153).

For additional sources of "Saint Narcissus," see Grover Smith, 34–35 and Gottlieb, 54–56.

5. References to Massine and the Ballets Russes are in *The Letters,* 292, 319, 523, and 529.

6. "Dramatis Personae," *Criterion* (April 1923): 306.

7. "A Commentary," *Criterion* 3, no. 10 (1925): 161–63.

8. "London Letter," *Dial* (August 1921): 214.

9. "London Letter," *Dial* (October 1921).

10. "The Ballet," *Criterion* (April 1925): 441–43.

11. "The Beating of a Drum," *The Nation and Athenaeum* (6 October 1923): 12.

12. In the September 1918 issue of the *Egoist*, Eliot concluded a review of Wyndham Lewis's novel *Tarr* with the following observation: "The artist I believe is more *primitive*, as well as more civilized, than his contemporaries, his experience is deeper than civilization, and he only uses the phenomena of civilization in expressing it" (*Selected Essays* 106).

13. Since Nijinsky's version caused such an uproar among the French intelligentsia, it is likely that Eliot was familiar with Jacques Rivière's two essays for *La Nouvelle Revue Française,* which vividly described the modernity of Nijinsky's ballet and the horror of its violence (Howarth 235–36). Eliot would have applauded what Rivière described as Nijinsky's anti-romantic movement vocabulary, especially the latter's rejection of individualism and a transcendent idealism. According to Rivière, "Nijinsky's movement closes over the emotion; it arrests and contains it. . . . The body is no longer a means of escape for the soul . . . but by the very resistance that it offers to the soul, becomes completely permeated by it" (quoted, Rivière 120).

14. "London Letter," *Dial* (October 1921): 453.

15. "The Possibility of a Poetic Drama," *Dial* (November 1920): 447.

16. Eliot had singled out Davies in a 1926 essay, including him among those poets who "had that strange gift . . . for turning thought into feeling" (*On Poetry and Poets* 136). For a more elaborate discussion of Davies's role in "Burnt Norton," see Salamon, "The Orchestration of 'Burnt Norton, II,'" 50–65; Bernstein, "Dance in the *Four Quartets,"* 230–61; and Blamires, 18.

17. The still point has a rich critical history. Some critics have heard its Dantean echoes, especially in the "Paradiso"'s vision of God as "a brilliant point of light where all time is present and about which nine choirs of angels, impelled by divine love revolve at varying speeds" (Bernstein, "Dancing in *Four Quartets*" 248–49). Hugh Kenner compares the still point to a wheel, "the exact center of which is motionless, whatever the velocity of the rim" (254). Morris Weitz focuses on its thematic implications as a meditation on time and timelessness. According to him, Eliot

held a Christian, neo-Platonic theory of time, which was "essentially an Immanence doctrine according to which the Eternal or Timeless is the creative source of the flux or temporal." The flux is real "but its reality is derived from and sustained by the more ultimate reality of the Eternal" (142). ("Only through time time is conquered," 90.) Weitz argued further that Eliot equated the still point with Heraclitus's logos, which he then interpreted as a symbol of the Christian God or Incarnation. God as the still point was a variation of the Greek concept of an Unmoved Mover: One who does not move Himself but was the source of all movement.

18. For an elaboration of Elyot's treatise, see Major, "Elyot's Moralization of the Dance," 27–36; and Salamon, "A Gloss on 'Daunsinge': Sir Thomas Elyot and T. S. Eliot's *Four Quartets,*" 584–605. Major contrasts Elyot's emphasis on the moral virtues of dance with Davies's more aesthetic approach in *The Orchestra*. Salamon draws out the differences between Eliot's attitude toward dance in "East Coker" with his namesake's humanist treatment in *The Boke*. According to her, Eliot used Elyot's words in this passage as conscious archaisms to evoke the past and "give it a gracious, honorable meaning." But he also knew the effect was "patently dated." For Salamon, anyone acquainted with *The Governour* would know the shadowy figures are not Elyot's aristocratic dancers: "His courtly couples move in handfast pairs at a stately pace down a late medieval hall to the tune of shawm and rebeck, not pipe and drum . . . loam feet and rustic laughter are not dignified, the coupling of man and woman is not a sacrament, feet rising and falling are not commodious but vaguely ominous" (599).

19. Much earlier, in the 1917 poem "A Cooking Egg," Eliot had alluded to Weber's music for *Le Spectre de la rose, An Invitation to the Dance*.

D. H. Lawrence

1. *The Trespasser, Aaron's Rod,* and *Kangaroo* are the three novels without dance scenes. *The Lost Girl* and *Boy in the Bush* do contain dance, but not significantly enough to be treated separately.

2. Lawrence first mentions phallic consciousness in a 1915 letter to Bertrand Russell in which he states his belief in "another seat of consciousness which exists in us independently of the ordinary mental consciousness" (*Letters* 2:393–94). Birkin in *Women in Love* calls it the "great dark knowledge you can't have in your head. . . . It is death to one's

self—but it is the coming into being of another" (36). Other references to the term are in "Study of Thomas Hardy" (*Phx* 398–516), *"A Propos of Lady Chatterley's Lover"* (*Phx II* 487–518), and *Fantasia of the Unconscious.*

3. For Lawrence's account of his friendship with Magnus, the reader is referred to his "Introduction to 'Memoirs of the Foreign Legion'" (*Phx II* 303–61).

4. In Beardsley's "The Peacock Skirt," for example, Salomé wears an elaborate headdress made of peacock feathers, and in this picture as well as "The Eyes of Herod" an actual peacock appears.

5. In 1913 Lawrence wrote a friend from Lerici, Italy, requesting some books: "I love travels and other raw philosophy and when you can lend me books about Greek religions and the rise of Greek Drama, or Egyptian influences—or things like that—I love them. I got a fearful lot out of a scrubby book *Art and Ritual*—one of the Universal Knowledge Shilling series. It is stupidly put, but it lets one in for an idea that helps one immensely" (*Letters* 1:250).

6. José Limón's classic *The Moor's Pavane* immediately comes to mind by Schorer's analogy. The dance, a powerful distillation of Shakespeare's *Othello*, consists of a quartet (as in *Women in Love*) whose members move across the stage in symmetrical and shifting patterns which analogue their shifting loyalties to each other.

7. The dance in the "style of the Russian ballet" has some basis in real life. The "real" Hermione, Lady Ottoline Morrell, according to Garafola, "opened her wardrobes of Oriental clothing to Bloomsbury friends . . . who danced pianola versions of the Polovtsian dances and Schéhérazade at her Thursday evening parties" (322). Lawrence was obviously parodying the way the Ballets Russes sparked the hedonist fantasies of the Bloomsbury crowd.

8. Jaques-Dalcroze claimed he gave his students musical *experience* rather than musical *knowledge* through eurythmics. The emphasis on the felt rather than the known would have appealed to Lawrence.

9. According to Vivas, bulls are "semiotic symbols throughout many cultures of male potency, of fruitfulness." Why Gudrun attacks emasculated "bullocks" is one of those "fascinating, but obscure" elements in Lawrence's symbolism that does not lend itself entirely to rational explanation (245).

W. C. Williams

1. See "The Poem as a Field of Action," *Selected Essays,* 280–91.

2. See Stephen Cushman, *William Carlos Williams and the Meaning of Measure,* for a thorough analysis of the poet's method of lineation in his nonmetrical verse. Williams's numerous references to the word "measure" are often contradictory or confusing, according to Cushman, because of the poet's tendency to not distinguish between two entirely different meanings of the word. Williams often used "measure" in its specific technical sense of signifying pseudomusical divisions in verse. But he also meant "measure" as "meet" or fitting, appropriate, commensurate. When used in the latter sense, Williams was generating poetic trope.

3. "I am told that it is my duty to write the biography of Martha Graham," he wrote in a letter to Alva Turner. But with Williams up to his neck in commitments, the project never materialized (*SL* 171).

4. Letter dated May 9, 1944, to Horace Gregory. Horace Gregory Papers, Syracuse University Library, Department of Special Collections.

5. Books 2, 3, 4, and 5 of *Paterson* were published in 1948, 1949, 1951, and 1958 respectively.

6. Analogous to the spring festival honoring Dionysus, the Eleusinian Mysteries (bequeathed to the ancestors of the Athenians by Demeter) were originally dance rites. Symbolic dramas which reenacted the myth, like the Attic tragedies, evolved later. The mimetic representations were said to put the participants in touch with divine power (as did the ecstatic dancing of Dionysus's followers) and as a result, mitigated their terror of death with intimations of an afterlife.

7. When asked in a 1962 interview if the satyrs represented "the element of freedom, of energy within the forms," Williams said, "Yes. The satyrs are understood as action, a dance. I always think of the Indians there" (Koehler 130).

8. The satyr's deformed foot also recalls the prose fragment at the end of book 1 which quotes from John Addington Symonds's *Studies of the Greek Poets* (1880). Symonds describes the lame or halting verses of Hipponax as being to poetry "what the dwarf or cripple is in human nature":

> Here again, by their acceptance of this halting meter, the Greeks displayed their acute sense of propriety, recognizing the harmony which subsists between crabbed verses and the distorted subjects with which they dealt—the vices and perversions of

humanity—as well as their agreement with the snarling spirit of the *satirist* [emphasis added]. Deformed verse was suited to deformed morality. (I, iii, 40)

Since one of *Paterson*'s themes is "the vices and perversions of humanity," Stephen Cushman persuasively argues that Williams felt justified in using "mutilated, crabbed verses, which range freely into prose and common speech" in the work (118). Cushman's reading of "to dance to a measure contrapuntally" as line-sentence counterpointing, refers to Williams's frequent use of enjambment and caesura, when sentences end in midline (22).

9. Like Eliot and Lawrence, Williams read Harrison's *Ancient Art and Ritual,* whose premise was based on Aristotle's statement in the *Poetics* that Greek tragedy grew out of the Dithyramb, or Greek spring festival honoring the god Dionysus. Williams was also no doubt aware of Aristotle's explanation of tragedy's "satyr-like" origins.

Even during the classical period, satyr plays were still performed and usually came after a trilogy of tragedies at the Dionysian festival. They resembled tragedies in form, but treated their Homeric legends grotesquely. The choruses from these plays were dressed to represent satyrs, and their language and movements were often obscene.

Bibliography

Ackroyd, Peter. *T. S. Eliot: A Life*. New York: Simon and Schuster, 1984.

Adams, Hazard. *The Book of Yeats's Poems*. Tallahassee: Florida State University Press, 1990.

Alldritt, Keith. *The Visual Imagination of D. H. Lawrence*. Evanston, Ill.: Northwestern University Press, 1971.

Archibald, Douglas. *Yeats*. Syracuse, N.Y.: Syracuse University Press, 1983.

Aristotle. *"Poetics."* Translated by S. H. Butcher. In *Problems in Aesthetics,* edited by Morris Weitz. New York: Macmillan, 1959. 20–24.

Balbert, Peter, and Phillip L. Marcus, eds. *D. H. Lawrence: A Centenary Consideration*. Ithaca, N.Y.: Cornell University Press, 1985.

Barthes, Roland. "The Death of the Author." In *Modern Literary Theory,* edited by Philip Rice and Patricia Waugh. London: Edward Arnold, 1992. 114–18.

Beaumont, Cyril. *Vaslav Nijinsky*. London: Beaumont, 1932.

Bergonzi, Bernard. *T. S. Eliot*. New York: Collier Books, 1972.

Bernstein, David. "The Story of Vaslav Nijinsky as a Source for T. S. Eliot's 'The Death of Saint Narcissus.'" *Hebrew University Studies in Literature* 4 (1976): 71–104.

———. "Dance in the *Four Quartets*." *Hebrew University Studies in Literature* 9, no. 2 (1981): 230–61.

Blair, Fredrika. *Isadora: Portrait of the Artist as a Woman*. New York: McGraw-Hill, 1986.

Blamires, Harry. *Word Unheard: A Guide through Eliot's* Four Quartets. London: Methuen, 1969.

Bloom, Harold. *Yeats*. New York: Oxford University Press, 1970.

Bornstein, George. *Transformations of Romanticism in Yeats, Eliot, and Stevens*. Chicago: University of Chicago Press, 1976.

Bowra, C. M. *The Heritage of Symbolism*. London: Macmillan, 1959.

Bradbury, Malcolm, and James McFarlane. "Movements, Magazines, and Manifestos: The Succession from Naturalism." In

Modernism: 1890–1930, edited by Malcolm Bradbury and James
          McFarlane. New York: Penguin, 1976. 191–205.

Bradford, Curtis. *Yeats at Work.* Carbondale: Southern Illinois
          University Press, 1965.

Brandabur, A. M. "The Ritual Corn Harvest Scene in *The Rainbow.*"
          D. H. Lawrence Review 6 (1973): 284–302.

Breslin, James E. B. *William Carlos Williams: An American Artist.*
          Chicago: University of Chicago Press, 1985.

Brooks, Cleanth. *The Well Wrought Urn: Studies in the Structure of
          Poetry.* New York: Harcourt, Brace, 1947.

Bush, Ronald. *T. S. Eliot: The Modernist in History.* Cambridge:
          Cambridge University Press, 1991.

Caldwell, Helen. *Michio Ito: The Dancer and His Dances.* Berkeley:
          University of California Press, 1977.

Campbell, Joseph. *The Hero with a Thousand Faces.* Princeton, N.J.:
          Princeton University Press, 1971.

Cherniavsky, Felix. "Maud Allan, Part III: Two Years of Triumph,
          1908–1909." *Dance Chronicle.* 7, no. 2 (1984): 119–58.

Copeland, Roger. "Towards a Sexual Politics of Contemporary
          Dance." *Contact Quarterly* (Spring/Summer 1982): 45–50.

Copeland, Roger, and Marshall Cohen, eds. *What Is Dance?: Readings
          in Theory and Criticism.* New York: Oxford University Press,
          1983.

Crane, Hart. *The Letters of Hart Crane.* Edited by Brom Weber.
          Berkeley: University of California Press, 1965.

Croce, Arlene. *Going to the Dance.* New York: Knopf, 1982.

Cullingford, Elizabeth. *Yeats's Poems 1919–1935: A Casebook.* London:
          Macmillan, 1984.

Cushman, Keith. *D. H. Lawrence at Work.* Charlottesville: University
          Press of Virginia, 1978.

Cushman, Stephen. *William Carlos Williams and the Meaning of
          Measure.* New Haven, Conn.: Yale University Press, 1985.

Davies, Sir John. *Orchestra, or a Poem of Dancing.* Edited by E. M. W.
          Tillyard. London: Chatto and Windus, 1947.

de Man, Paul. *Allegories of Reading.* New Haven, Conn.: Yale
          University Press, 1979.

de Valois, Ninette. *Come Dance with Me: A Memoir.* London: Hamish
          Hamilton, 1957.

Donne, John. *The Complete English Poems.* Edited by A. J. Smith.
          Harmondsworth, Middlesex, England: Penguin, 1984. 287–301.

Duncan, Isadora. *My Life*. 1927. Reprint, New York: Award Books, 1966.

———. *The Art of the Dance*. New York: Theater Arts, 1928.

Eliot, T. S. "Tradition and the Individual Talent." 1917. Reprinted in *Selected Essays*. New York: Harcourt, Brace, 1950.

———. "The Possibility of a Poetic Drama." *Dial* (November 1920): 441–47.

———. "London Letter." *Dial* (July 1921): 214.

———. "London Letter." *Dial* (October 1921): 452–53.

———. "Dramatis Personae." *Criterion* (April 1923): 303–6.

———. "The Beating of a Drum." *The Nation and Athenaeum* (6 October 1923): 11–12.

———. "A Commentary." *Criterion* (October 1924): 1–3.

———. "A Commentary." *Criterion* (January 1925): 161–63.

———. "The Ballet." *Criterion* (April 1925): 441–43.

———. "Sir John Davies." *On Poetry and Poets*. 1926. Reprint, London: Faber, 1990.

———. "A Dialogue on Dramatic Poetry." 1928. Reprinted in *Selected Essays*. New York: Harcourt, Brace, 1950. 31–45.

———. *Selected Poems*. 1930. Reprint, New York: Harcourt, Brace, Jovanovich, 1964.

———. *The Use of Poetry and the Use of Criticism*. London: Faber, 1933.

———. "Four Elizabethan Dramatists." 1934. Reprinted in *Selected Essays*. New York: Harcourt, Brace, 1950. 91–99.

———. "The Music of Poetry." 1942. *On Poetry and Poets*. London: Faber, 1990. 26–38.

———. *Four Quartets*. 1943. Reprint, New York: Harcourt, Brace, Jovanovich, 1971.

———. *Selected Essays*. New York: Harcourt, Brace, 1950.

———. *The Complete Poems and Plays*. New York: Harcourt, Brace, 1952.

———. *The Waste Land: A Facsimile and Transcript of the Original Drafts*. Edited by Valerie Eliot. New York: Harcourt, Brace, Jovanovich, 1971.

———. *The Letters of T. S. Eliot: 1898–1922*. Vol. 1. Edited by Valerie Eliot. New York: Harcourt, Brace, Jovanovich, 1988.

———. *On Poetry and Poets*. London: Faber, 1990.

Ellis, Havelock. "The Dance of Life." In *The Dance Anthology*, edited by Cobbett Steinberg. New York: New American Library, 1980. 238–54.

174

Ellmann, Richard. *The Identity of Yeats.* New York: Oxford University Press, 1954.

Elsbree, Langdon. "D. H. Lawrence, Homo Ludens, and the Dance." *D. H. Lawrence Review* (1968): 1–30.

———. "The Purest and Most Perfect Form of Play: Some Novelists and the Dance." *Criticism* (Fall 1972): 361–72.

Engleberg, Edward. *The Vast Design: Patterns in W. B. Yeats's Aesthetic.* Toronto: University of Toronto Press, 1964.

Feder, Lillian. *Ancient Myth in Modern Poetry.* Princeton, N.J.: Princeton University Press, 1971.

Forster, E. M. "A Shrine for Diaghilev." *Observer* (25 December 1955).

Foster, John Burt, Jr. *Heirs to Dionysus: A Nietzschean Current in Literary Modernism.* Princeton, N.J.: Princeton University Press, 1981.

Frazer, Sir James. *The Golden Bough: A Study in Magic and Religion.* Vol. 5. New York: Macmillan, 1951.

Fuller, Loïe. *Fifteen Years of a Dancer's Life.* Brooklyn: Dance Horizon Republication, 1915.

Gajdusek, Robert E. "A Reading of *The White Peacock.*" In *A D. H. Lawrence Miscellany,* edited by Harry T. Moore. Carbondale: Southern Illinois University Press, 1959. 188–203.

Garafola, Lynn. *Diaghilev's Ballets Russes.* New York: Oxford University Press, 1989.

Gardner, Helen. *The Composition of the* Four Quartets. New York: Oxford University Press, 1978.

Gilbert, Sandra M., and Susan Gubar. *Sex Changes.* Vol. 2 of *No Man's Land: The Place of the Woman Writer in the Twentieth Century.* New Haven, Conn.: Yale University Press, 1989.

Goodman, Nelson. "The Role of Notations." In *What Is Dance?: Readings in Theory and Criticism,* edited by Roger Copeland and Marshall Cohen. New York: Oxford University Press, 1983. 399–410.

Gordon, Lyndall. *Eliot's Early Years.* New York: The Noonday Press, 1977.

———. *Eliot's New Life.* New York: The Noonday Press, 1988.

Gottlieb, Sidney. "Eliot's 'The Death of Saint Narcissus' and Herbert's 'Affliction.'" *George Herbert Journal* 9, no. 2 (1986): 54–56.

Graham, Martha. *Blood Memory: An Autobiography.* New York: Washington Square Press, 1991.

Gregory, Horace. Papers. Syracuse University Library, Department of Special Collections.

Hanna, Judith Lynne. *Dance, Sex, and Gender.* Chicago: University of Chicago Press, 1988.

Harrison, Jane. *Ancient Art and Ritual.* London: Williams and Norgate, 1913.

Hodson, Millicent. "Nijinsky's Choreographic Method: Visual Sources for *Le Sacre du printemps.*" *Dance Research Journal* 18 (1986–87): 7–15.

Howarth, Herbert. *Notes on Some Figures behind T. S. Eliot.* Boston: Houghton Mifflin, 1964.

Jaques-Dalcroze, Emile. *The Eurhythmics of Jaques-Dalcroze.* London: Constable, 1912.

Jeffares, A. Norman. *A New Commentary on the Poems of W. B. Yeats.* Stanford, Calif.: Stanford University Press, 1984.

———. *W. B. Yeats: A New Biography.* New York: Farrar, 1988.

Jowitt, Deborah. *Time and the Dancing Image.* Berkeley: University of California Press, 1988.

Kendall, Elizabeth. *Where She Danced: The Birth of American Art-Dance.* Berkeley: University of California Press, 1979.

Kennedy, Richard S. *Dreams in the Mirror: A Biography of E. E. Cummings.* New York: Liveright, 1980.

Kenner, Hugh. *The Invisible Poet: T. S. Eliot.* London: Methuen, 1959.

Kermode, Frank. "Poet and Dancer before Diaghilev." In *What Is Dance?: Readings in Theory and Criticism,* edited by Roger Copeland and Marshall Cohen. New York: Oxford University Press, 1983. 145–60.

———. *Romantic Image.* London: Ark Paperbacks, 1986.

Kirstein, Lincoln. *Nijinsky Dancing.* New York: Knopf, 1975.

Koehler, Stanley. "The Art of Poetry: William Carlos Williams." *Paris Review* 8, no. 32 (1964): 130.

Lawrence, D. H. *The White Peacock.* 1911. Reprint, New York: Penguin, 1987.

———. *Sons and Lovers.* 1913. Reprint, New York: Viking, 1969.

———. *The Rainbow.* 1915. Reprint, New York: Penguin, 1984.

———. *The Lost Girl.* 1920. Reprint, London: Grafton, 1981.

———. *Women in Love.* 1920. Reprint, New York: Viking, 1960.

———. *Fantasia of the Unconscious and Psychoanalysis of the Unconscious.* 1923. Reprint, New York: Penguin, 1977.

———. *Studies in Classic American Literature.* 1924. Reprint, New York: Penguin, 1977.

———. *Plumed Serpent.* 1926. Reprint, Cambridge: Cambridge University Press, 1987.

———. *Phoenix: The Posthumous Papers of D. H. Lawrence.* Edited by Edward D. McDonald. 1936. Reprint, New York: Penguin, 1985.

———. *Selected Essays.* 1950. Reprint, New York: Penguin, 1986.

———. *Mornings in Mexico and Etruscan Places.* London: Heinemann, 1956.

———. *Lady Chatterley's Lover.* New York: Penguin, 1959.

———. *The Collected Letters of D. H. Lawrence.* Vol. 1. Edited by Harry T. Moore. New York: Viking, 1962.

———. *Phoenix II: Uncollected, Unpublished, and Other Prose Works.* Edited by Warren Roberts and Harry T. Moore. 1968. Reprint, New York: Penguin, 1978.

———. *D. H. Lawrence in Italy: Twilight in Italy, Sea and Sardinia, Etruscan Places.* New York: Viking, 1972.

———. *The Letters of D. H. Lawrence.* Vol. 1: September 1901–May 1913. Edited by James T. Boulton. Cambridge: Cambridge University Press, 1979.

———. *The Letters of D. H. Lawrence.* Vol. 2: June 1913–October 1916. Edited by George J. Zytaruk and James T. Boulton. Cambridge: Cambridge University Press, 1981.

———. *The Complete Short Stories.* Vol. 1. New York: Penguin, 1985.

Lawson, Joan. *European Folk Dance.* New York: Arno Press, 1980.

Loewinsohn, Ron. "'Fools Have Big Wombs': William Carlos Williams's *Kora in Hell.*" *Essays in Literature* 4 (1977): 221–38.

Ludington, Townsend. *John Dos Passos: A Twentieth Century Odyssey.* New York: E. P. Dutton, 1980.

Lynch, David. *Yeats: The Poetics of the Self.* Chicago: University of Chicago Press, 1979.

Magriel, Paul, ed. *Chronicles of the American Dance from the Shakers to Martha Graham.* New York: DaCapo Press, 1976.

Major, John D. "Elyot's Moralization of the Dance." *Studies in the Renaissance* 5 (1958): 27–36

Mallarmé, Stéphane. *Selected Prose Poems, Essays, and Letters.* Translated by Bradford Cook. Baltimore: The Johns Hopkins University Press, 1956.

———. *Selected Poetry and Prose.* Translated by Mary Ann Caws. New York: New Directions, 1982.

———. "Ballets." In *What is Dance?: Readings in Theory and Criticism,* edited by Roger Copeland and Marshall Cohen. New York: Oxford University Press, 1983. 111–15.

Mariani, Paul. *William Carlos Williams: A New World Naked*. New
York: McGraw-Hill, 1982.

Mayer, John T. *T. S. Eliot's Silent Voices*. New York: Oxford University
Press, 1989.

McWhirter, David B. "The Rhythm of the Body in Yeats's 'Nineteen
Hundred and Nineteen.'" *College Literature* 13, no. 1 (1986):
44–54.

Melchiori, Giorgio. *The Whole Mystery of Art: Pattern into Poetry in the
Work of W. B. Yeats*. Westport, Conn.: Greenwood Press, 1979.

Meyers, Jeffrey. *D. H. Lawrence: A Biography*. New York: Vintage,
1992.

Miki, Roy. *The Prepoetics of William Carlos Williams:* Kora in Hell. Ann
Arbor, Mich.: UMI Research Press, 1983.

Miller, J. Hillis. *Six Poets of Reality*. Cambridge, Mass.: Harvard
University Press, 1965.

———. *The Linguistic Moment from Wordsworth to Stevens*. Princeton,
N.J.: Princeton University Press, 1985.

Munro, John M. *Arthur Symons*. New York: Twayne, 1969.

Nelson, Karen. "Bringing Fokine to Light." *Dance Research Journal* 16
(1984): 3–12.

Nehls, Edward. *D. H. Lawrence: A Composite Biography*. Vol. 1:
1885–1919. Madison: University of Wisconsin Press, 1957.

Nietzsche, Friedrich. *The Birth of Tragedy*. Translated by Walter
Kaufman. New York: Vintage, 1967.

———. *Thus Spoke Zarathustra*. Translated by R. J. Hollingdale. New
York: Penguin, 1969.

Ortega y Gassett, José. *The Dehumanization of Art, and Other
Writings on Art and Culture*. New York: Doubleday, 1956.

Pall, Santosh. "The Dancer in Yeats." *Studies: An Irish Quarterly
Review* 65 (1976): 113–27.

Parrish, Stephen M. *A Concordance to the Poems of W. B. Yeats*.
Programmer, James A. Painter. Ithaca, N.Y.: Cornell University
Press, 1963. 181–82.

Patmore, Brigid. *My Friends When Young*. London: Heinemann, 1968.

Paul, Sherman. *The Music of Survival: A Biography of a Poem by
William Carlos Williams*. Urbana: University of Illinois Press,
1968.

———. "A Sketchbook of the Artist in His Thirty-Fourth Year:
William Carlos Williams's *Kora in Hell: Improvisations.*" In *The
Shaken Realist: Essays in Modern Literature in Honor of Frederick*

J. Hoffman, edited by Melvin J. Friedman and John B. Vickery. Baton Rouge: Louisiana State University Press, 1970. 21–44.

Pinciss, G. M. "A Dancer for Mr. Yeats." *Educational Theater Journal* 21, no. 4 (1969): 386–91.

Pinkney, Tony. *D. H. Lawrence and Modernism.* Iowa City: University of Iowa Press, 1990.

Porter, Laurence M. *The Crisis of French Symbolism.* Ithaca, N.Y.: Cornell University Press, 1990.

Praz, Mario. *The Romantic Agony.* Oxford: Oxford University Press, 1951.

Priddin, Deirdre. *The Art of Dance in French Literature.* London: Adam and Charles Black, 1952.

Ragussis, Michael. *The Subterfuge of Art: Language and the Romantic Tradition.* Baltimore: Johns Hopkins University Press, 1978.

Rambert, Marie. *Quicksilver: The Autobiography of Marie Rambert.* London: Macmillan, 1972.

Rapp, Carl. *William Carlos Williams and Romantic Idealism.* Hanover, Md.: Brown University Press, 1984.

Riddel, Joseph N. "The Wanderer and the Dance: William Carlos Williams's Early Poetics." In *The Shaken Realist: Essays in Modern Literature in Honor of Frederick J. Hoffman,* edited by Melvin J. Friedman and John B. Vickery. Baton Rouge: Louisiana State University Press, 1970. 45–71.

———. *The Inverted Bell: Modernism and the Counterpoetics of William Carlos Williams.* Baton Rouge: Louisiana State University Press, 1974.

Rivière, Jacques. "Le Sacre du Printemps." In *What Is Dance?: Readings in Theory and Criticism,* edited by Roger Copeland and Marshall Cohen. New York: Oxford University Press, 1983. 115–22.

Rodgers, Audrey T. *The Universal Drum: Dance Imagery in the Poetry of Crane, Eliot, Roethke, and Williams.* University Park: Pennsylvania State University Press, 1979.

Rosenthal, M. L., and Sally M. Gall. *The Modern Poetic Sequence: The Genius of Poetry.* Oxford: Oxford University Press, 1983.

Rosenzweig, Paul. "The Making of Ursula Brangwen's Identity: The Pattern of the Ritual Scenes in *The Rainbow.*" *University of Mississippi Studies in English* 6 (1988) 206–27.

Ross, Adam. *The Failure of Modernism: Symptoms of American Poetry.* New York: Columbia University Press, 1986.

Ross, Donald, Jr. "Stylistic Contrasts in Yeats's Byzantium Poems."   179
   Language and Style 9 (1976): 293–305.
Rust, Frances. *Dance in Society*. London: Routledge and Kegan Paul,
   1969.
Sachs, Curt. *World History of the Dance*. Translated by Bessie
   Schönberg. New York: Norton, 1937.
Sagar, Keith. *The Art of D. H. Lawrence*. Cambridge: Cambridge
   University Press, 1966.
St. Denis, Ruth. *An Unfinished Life*. New York: Harper and Brothers,
   1939.
Salamon, Linda Bradley. "A Gloss on 'Daunsinge': Sir Thomas Elyot
   and T. S. Eliot's *Four Quartets.*" *ELH* 40 (1973): 584–605.
———. "The Orchestration of 'Burnt Norton, II.'" *University of
   Toronto Quarterly* 45 (1975): 50–65.
Sankey, Benjamin. *A Companion to William Carlos Williams's* Paterson.
   Berkeley: University of California Press, 1971.
Schmidt, Peter. *William Carlos Williams, the Arts, and Literary
   Tradition*. Baton Rouge: Louisiana State University Press, 1988.
Schorer, Mark. "*Women in Love* and Death." In *D. H. Lawrence: A
   Collection of Critical Essays,* edited by Mark Spilka. Englewood
   Cliffs, N.J.: Prentice-Hall, 1963. 50–60.
Schwartz, Sanford. *The Matrix of Modernism: Pound, Eliot, and Early
   Twentieth-Century Thought*. Princeton, N.J.: Princeton
   University Press, 1985.
Shaw, Mary Lewis. "Ephemeral Signs: Apprehending the Idea Through
   Poetry and Dance." *Dance Research Journal* 20 (1988): 3–9.
Sheets-Johnstone, Maxine, ed. *Illuminating Dance: Philosophical
   Explorations*. Associated University Presses: London and
   Toronto, 1984.
Shelton, Suzanne. *Divine Dancer: A Biography of Ruth St. Denis*. New
   York: Doubleday, 1981.
Skaff, William. *The Philosophy of T. S. Eliot: From Skepticism to a
   Surrealist Poetic*. Philadelphia: University of Pennsylvania Press,
   1986.
Smith, Grover. *T. S. Eliot's Poetry and Plays: A Study in Sources and
   Meanings*. Chicago: University of Chicago Press, 1956.
Sommer, Sally R. "Loïe Fuller's Art of Music and Light." *Dance
   Chronicle* (1981): 389–401.
Southam, B. C. *A Student's Guide to the Selected Poems of T. S. Eliot*.
   5th edition. London: Faber, 1990.

180

Spears, Monroe K. *Dionysus and the City.* New York: Oxford University Press, 1970.

Spencer, Charles, and Philip Dyer. *The World of Diaghilev.* Chicago: Henry Regnery, 1974.

Symons, Arthur. "The World as Ballet." In *The Dance Anthology,* edited by Cobbett Steinberg. New York: New American Library, 1980. 346–50.

Traversi, Derek. *T. S. Eliot: The Longer Poems.* New York: Harcourt, Brace, Jovanovich, 1976.

Unterecker, John. *A Reader's Guide to William Butler Yeats.* New York: Octagon Books, 1983.

———, ed. *Yeats : A Collection of Critical Essays.* Englewood Cliffs, N.J.: Prentice-Hall, 1963.

Valéry, Paul. "Dance and the Soul." In *Paul Valéry: An Anthology,* selected by James R. Lawler. Princeton, N.J.: Princeton University Press, 1977. 291–326.

———. "Philosophy of the Dance." In *What Is Dance?: Readings in Theory and Criticism,* edited by Roger Copeland and Marshall Cohen. New York: Oxford University Press, 1983. 55–65.

Vivas, Eliseo. *D. H. Lawrence: The Failure and Triumph of Art.* Evanston, Ill.: Northwestern University Press, 1960.

Wagner-Martin, Linda. *The Prose of William Carlos Williams.* Middleton, Conn.: Wesleyan University Press, 1970.

Wain, John, ed. *Interpretations: Essays on Twelve English Poems.* London: Routledge and Kegan Paul, 1972.

Wallace, Emily. "The Satyrs' Abstract and Brief Chronicle of Our Time." *William Carlos Williams Review* 9, nos. 1–2 (1983): 136–55.

Weitz, Morris. "T. S. Eliot: Time as a Mode of Salvation." In *T. S. Eliot's* Four Quartets: *A Casebook,* edited by Bernard Bergonzi. London: Macmillan, 1969.

Wheelwright, Philip. *Metaphor and Reality.* Bloomington: Indiana University Press, 1975.

Williams, William Carlos. "America, Whitman, and the Art of Poetry." *Poetry Journal* 8 (November 1917): 27–36.

———. *The Selected Poems of William Carlos Williams.* 1917. Reprint, New York: New Directions, 1968.

———. *The Doctor Stories.* 1932. Reprint, New York: New Directions, 1984.

———. *The Farmers' Daughters: The Collected Stories of William Carlos Williams.* 1932. Reprint, New York: New Directions, 1961.

———. *In the American Grain.* 1933. Reprint, New York: New Directions, 1956.

———. *Paterson.* 1946–58. Reprint, New York:New Directions , 1969.

———. *The Autobiography of William Carlos Williams.* 1951. Reprint, New York: New Directions, 1967.

———. *Selected Essays.* 1954. Reprint, New York: New Directions, 1969.

———. *The Selected Letters of William Carlos Williams.* Edited by John T. Thirlwall. 1957. Reprint, New York: New Directions, 1985.

———. *I Wanted to Write a Poem.* Edited by Edith Heal. Boston: Beacon Press, 1958

———. *Pictures From Brueghel and Other Poems.* New York: New Directions, 1962.

———. *Imaginations.* Edited by Webster Schott. New York: New Directions, 1970.

———. *The Collected Poems of William Carlos Williams.* Vol. 1: 1909–39. Edited by A. Walton Litz and Christopher MacGowan. New York: New Directions, 1986.

Woolf, Leonard. *Beginning Again: An Autobiography of the Years 1911–1918.* New York: Harcourt, Brace, Jovanovich, 1963.

Yeats, John Butler. *Letters to His Son and Others.* Edited by Joseph Hone. New York: E. P. Dutton, 1946.

Yeats, William Butler. *A Vision.* 1938. Reprint, New York: Macmillan, 1965.

———. *The Letters of W. B. Yeats.* Edited by Allan Wade. London: Macmillan, 1954.

———. *Autobiographies.* 1955. Reprint, New York: Macmillan, 1980.

———. *Mythologies.* 1959. Reprint, New York: Macmillan, 1989.

———. *The Secret Rose and Other Stories.* 1959. Reprint, New York: Macmillan, 1982.

———. *Essays and Introductions.* 1961. Reprint, New York: Macmillan, 1986.

———. *The Variorum Edition of the Plays of W. B. Yeats.* Edited by Russell K. Alspach. New York: Macmillan, 1966.

———. *Memoirs.* 1972. Reprint, New York: Macmillan, 1988.

———. *The Collected Poems of W. B. Yeats.* Edited by Richard J. Finneran. New York: Macmillan, 1989.

Index

A

B

Z